OFfBEAT
CAREERS

Off BEAT CAREERS

The Directory of Unusual Work

Al Sacharov

▲

TEN SPEED PRESS

1❿ **Ten Speed Press**
Post Office Box 7123
Berkeley, California 94707

First Printing 1988

Cover, book design and typography by
Fifth Street Design, Berkeley, California

Library of Congress Cataloging-in-Publication Data

Sacharov, Al.
  Offbeat careers.

  Includes index.
  1. Vocational guidance – United States – Directories.
2. United States – Occupations – Directories. I. Title.
HF5382.5.U5S22 1988   331.7′02′0973   88-2092
ISBN 089-815-240-2

Printed in the United States of America

  3 4 5   92 91

Contents

Preface, *ix*

Dedication

*To all of those who have taken or
will take the Insight Transformational
Seminars, and to Judy Kempa, who
helped
me find some insights of my own.*

Preface

Work is a four-letter word.

It's up to us to decide whether that four-letter word reads "drag" or "love."

Most work is a drag because it doesn't nourish our souls. It's the old square peg in a round hole routine. People find themselves trapped in dead-end jobs for a variety of reasons – parental pressure, hunger for prestige, or lack of courage to try something different. For most of us, it's a lot easier to complain about the present than to risk the future. But one of the saddest reasons for a person to stay stuck is not knowing the range of options that are available.

Offbeat Careers: The Directory of Unusual Work is intended to push back parameters for people. These are real jobs held by real people. The placement information is timely, accurate, and often no more than a phone call or letter away. Obviously, the positions that I write about are not for everyone. But even if you don't choose to work in the Antarctic, you can use this book to stimulate the thought process and open up more avenues on the road map of life.

We spend one-third of our lives working. That is a long time to be doing something that you don't like. The key is to trust your heart to move you where your talents can flourish. Once you realize that life means more than just punching a time clock, you will begin moving your energies into fields that really do need work. This old world will really spin when work becomes a joyous expression of the soul.

For those of you who can use this book to find your special niche in life, then it is my honor and privilege to be of service to you. May you read it while whistling the tune, "Nice work if you can get it, and you can get it if you try."

1 Acupuncturist

Imagine that the body is more than just an assemblage of organs, arms, and legs. Imagine that it is balanced and nourished by a flow of energy through all of its parts, energy that can sometimes be blocked or bottlenecked, thus leading to disease. This concept of energy flow has been at the heart of oriental medicine for centuries, and the guiding of this energy for harmonious results is the goal of the Eastern medical discipline known as acupuncture.

Acupuncture involves more than just the common perception of placing needles throughout the body. It also encompasses a total philosophy of mind, body, and spirit. In Eastern thought, good health means more than absence of disease. Since 1972, the study and practice of acupuncture has been expanding in the United States, attracting practitioners who seek to complement the Western approach to medicine which involves more direct methods, such as surgery, to remove specific diseased tissues. According to acupuncturist Dr. Haig Ignatius, "A person who has access to both types of medicine is getting great health care."

Those who seek to become acupuncturists should do some initial readings in Eastern philosophy to expose themselves to its teachings. A visit to a practicing acupuncturist and an actual acupuncture treatment are also recommended. The next step would be to apply to an accredited school. One can be found by writing to the:

1

**National Council of Acupuncture Schools
and Colleges**
P.O. Box 954
Columbia, MD 21044

Schools have different admission policies. Some accept students out of high school while others require a college degree with emphasis on life sciences and/or clinical experience working with patients.

While at school, students focus on both the philosophy and the practice of oriental medicine. The energy pathways of the body, called meridians, are explored and their intersections are identified. These intersections are where the needles (which are as fine as three human hairs) are inserted to direct the body's energy, which is called the *chi.*

Upon graduation, an acupuncturist needs to consider the licensing requirements that exist for each state. Some states allow acupuncturists to practice independently while others require a physician's supervision. Regulations are becoming more standardized as acupuncture becomes more widely accepted.

Since each person's problems are unique, the study and practice of medicine will always be dynamic. Acupuncturists accept this need to constantly expand one's awareness and compassion. Indeed, as the ancient Chinese philosopher Lao Tsu once said, "Keep empty and you will be filled."

2 Air Courier

If you can travel light, you can travel far as an air courier. Most major cities have firms that employ individuals on a freelance basis to shepherd packages around the country, sometimes even around the world. These firms are listed under Air Courier Service in the Yellow Pages. They offer 40 to 70 percent reductions in air fare to individuals in exchange for their checked-in luggage rights. For instance, if you are interested in flying to Hong Kong from New York City as an air courier, you would contact a firm such as Now Voyager in Manhattan and ask when the next flight is open that suits your schedule. You would then go to a New York airport with carry-on luggage only. The courier firm would arrange to have its package checked aboard as tagged luggage. This package may contain machine parts, dress patterns, computer chips, or other commercial products. When the airplane reaches Hong Kong, a representative of the firm would be waiting to claim the package at the luggage ramp.

The main advantage of an air courier jaunt is its cheap price, but the disadvantage is being limited to only one personal bag. Also, you should be quite clear about whether the return trip is included in the fare, and whether that trip will also involve a delivery. Time flexibility is a must, making actors, restaurant workers, and freelancers ideal for this position. If a toothbrush and a change of underwear are all that you

3

need, then the friendly skies can also become very affordable.

3 Animal Trainer

A person does not have to be Dr. Doolittle to talk to the animals. People around the country are earning their livings by training and grooming dogs, cats, birds, and other more exotic animals.

Dog obedience training is the field with the largest growth potential. Dog owners who are tired of having their pets slobbering over their guests and mangling furniture often opt for the services of experienced handlers to help put the "good" in "good dog."

To be a successful trainer, you must first of all like animals, according to Terry Martin, owner of the Animal Learning Center in New York City. Novice trainers usually develop their skills by joining the armed forces and attending schools run by the military or by apprenticing themselves to trainers who are established in the civilian world. Trainers can be located either through the Yellow Pages or magazines such as *Dog World*. A nationally known school that offers 3- to 12-month-long courses in all phases of dog training is the:

Malibu Pet Hotel and Training Center
107 Guy Lombardo Avenue
Freeport, NY 11520

As might be expected, newcomers to the field start by cleaning kennels and then proceed to learn the necessary skills of working with animals and their owners. "Those persons who are truly successful in this field are able to relate to both dogs and people," Martin said.

5

They must also be willing to risk the occasional bite or scratch.

Ms. Martin estimated that a person could learn the basic techniques of dog handling after five months of effort. Following that it is a matter of continual learning on the job. Salaries and fees vary according to the different regions of the country and the intensity of the training. In major metropolitan areas, for instance, a well-trained guard dog can fetch up to $5,000, and a trainer can earn between $20,000 and $50,000 annually. For pet dogs, owners may pay up to $600 for a one-hour-per-week, two-month personalized course that covers such areas as housebreaking and basic obedience.

Other trainers devote their efforts to teaching obedience classes where larger groups of dogs and owners participate. Dog trainers can also supplement their income by breeding dogs, distributing pet care products, and maintaining boarding kennels.

Along these lines, you can consider the profession of pet grooming. The New York School of Dog Grooming, which is the nation's oldest such academy, offers a 300-hour, 10-week course that covers such topics as dog and cat show grooming, poodle clipping, dematting techniques, shampooing, and handling aggressive dogs (obviously ones who have not been trained!). The school can be contacted by writing to the:

New York School of Dog Grooming
248 East 34th Street
New York, NY 10016

It even offers dormitory space to accommodate students from all over the world. Most dog groomers are in business for themselves, so salaries depend on how a person commits his or her efforts to the profession. In general, however, an average dog clipping costs between $10 and $30.

If one is attracted to show business, there exists the more specialized field of training animals for movie and television work. Cindy Naples, who works for the San

Bernardino, California, firm of Jungle Exotics, said that a person should have a background in both cinematography and zoology and then apprentice to a trainer.

While on a set, an animal trainer earns the union rate of $21.55 per hour, but when there are no films being shot, the weekly salary as a keeper can be between $150 and $250 per week. "A person has to love animals in this line of work," Ms. Naples said. One attraction is the challenge of working with wild animals–gaining their trust and teaching them to function in the world of cameras and sets.

"Unlike circus animals, our animals must adapt to different requirements for each film," Ms. Naples noted. With the safety of both the animals and the film crew at stake, trainers of exotic animals simply cannot monkey around.

4 Antarctic Crew Member

For what earthly reason would someone want to subject themselves to 100-degree-below-zero weather, 24-hour-long nights, and physical isolation from the civilized world?

ADVENTURE!

If this is not reason enough, throw in a healthy salary and no chance to spend it, and you have the attraction of being an Antarctic crew member.

The frozen expanse of Antarctica is one of the world's most valuable natural laboratories. For that reason, in 1959, Great Britain, the United States, Australia, New Zealand, the Soviet Union, and Argentina signed a treaty that allows for scientific research to proceed unimpeded by nationalistic goals.

Each year hundreds of scientists travel to the permanent bases to conduct far-ranging experiments on climatology, the effects of pollution, and the possibility of developing Antarctic resources for the world. The plankton- and krill-rich waters, for instance, are potential sources of protein.

The United States maintains active year-round bases at McMurdo Sound, the South Pole, and Palmer Station. To supply logistical support for the teams of scientists, crews of workers are needed at all three sites. Approximately 500 workers are on the continent during the Antarctic summer (October to February), and the number drops to about 150 during the winter (March to September).

The agency that maintains the bases and hires individuals for polar work is the:

ITT Antarctic Services Division
621 Industrial Avenue
Paramus, NJ 07652

The folks who are needed at the South Pole are tradespeople who can keep the base going so that the scientists can operate. Specific abilities include plumbing, heating, cooking, managing records, housekeeping and maintenance, carpentry, communications, and mechanical skills. Both men and women are eligible. Preferably they should be in their twenties or thirties, psychologically well-adjusted, in excellent physical health, and with some education and training beyond high school.

As a safety survival skill, staffers are taught igloo construction, but actual accommodations are a bit more plush. Residents have small apartments with recreation facilities provided, along with radio contact to the "outside."

Based on an eight-hour workday, a crew member can expect to earn between $350 and $1,500 per week, meals included. Ah, but there is a catch—workers can stay at the most three seasons (18 months) before being rotated out. This is to keep people from developing cabin fever. The darkness, cold, and remoteness are drawbacks that discourage people from reapplying, and which also take their toll during the work season. Small peculiarities can become massive aggravations if people lose their sense of humor. It is possible, however, to reapply and some individuals do exactly that. With all the difficulties, one major advantage stands out—you can spend Christmas Eve at the South Pole and see just how far Santa does make it during the night!

5 Arborist

In many ways, the tree is man's best friend. It provides shade, fuel, fruit, and lumber. Also, like man's other best friend, it has a "bark."

It is the duty of the arborist, formerly known as a tree surgeon, to keep our "friends" healthy and thriving. According to Walter Dages, public relations director of the F.A. Bartlett Tree Expert Co. in Stamford, Connecticut, the profession actually has two major branches.

The first involves examining trees and deciding on the course of action that will benefit the tree in light of its intended purpose. Estimators visit property owners and assess the job that needs to be done, be it pruning, suppression of insects, or fertilization. Estimators usually have a college background in forestry or horticulture and also have good math and business skills, since they must determine expenses, the amount of time it will take to effect a treatment, and profit margins. "Labor expense is the big factor in tree care. Less than 1 percent of the cost involves actual materials," Dages said. Estimators are paid a commission based on job cost, and can earn between $20,000 and $100,000 per year.

The second aspect of tree care literally puts people out on a limb to actually do the job. Before a person works on a tree, he or she must be thoroughly conversant with safety procedures. This involves knowledge of the use of climbing ropes and saws, and an understanding of environmental rules pertaining to chemical spraying of trees. Once on a job, beginning arborists will work under the supervision of a foreman to gain additional expertise.

An arborist must have no fear of heights and must also enjoy working outdoors in all kinds of weather. For their efforts, arborists earn between $6 and $16 per hour. Perhaps because of the inherent dangers involved, there is a shortage of qualified workers in the field. Those who are interested can locate tree companies under the Tree Service heading in the Yellow Pages.

Closely related to the profession of arborist is that of the tree planter. Tree planters are hired by logging companies to replant tracts that have been clear-cut for timber or pulp. The actual planting involves making a hole with a mattock-shaped tool called a hoedad. The tree planter swings the hoedad overhead, drops it into the ground, puts in a seedling, tramps down the earth by foot, and then repeats the process several steps away. An experienced person can plant about 3,000 trees a day by this method.

Tree planters usually travel in crews from site to site, camping in trucks and vans on the work site. The same crew of 10 to 15 people may stay together for up to six months. Although the work is physically demanding, it is possible to earn about $100 per day while spending very little for living expenses. One firm that specializes in this profession is

Superior Forest Services
Route 85
Leslie, AR 72645

Again, the profession is for those who love working outdoors. The rugged life is compensated for by the close camaraderie that develops among crew members.

6 Art Restorer

"We're here to serve the artist, the poor bloody artist long since deceased, and the grandeur of his creation looking like a messed-up jigsaw puzzle, with all the values scrambled by the aging process and also by barbarous interference. You can never have enough qualities of intelligence to bring to that. But you do your damnedest to identify in the most servile way with the artist."

Thus did John M. Brealy in a *New Yorker* profile describe the role of the art conservator. Brealy is the chairman of the Department of Paintings Conservation at the Metropolitan Museum of Art in New York City, and is one of the master practitioners in the field–a field that requires patience, dedication, and training.

Artwork is prone to ills associated with aging. Pigments change color, paint chips away, canvas and paper slowly deteriorate. As Brealy noted, it is the mission of the art restorer to preserve for the public what the artist intended to convey, and to do so as unobtrusively as possible.

Art restorers must have an innate artistic sense, and need a college-level background in art history and chemistry. Many restorers start their careers volunteering their services to private restorers or to museums while they are still in school. These apprenticeships can last for several years, and they allow you to familiarize yourself with the restoration process. Duties entail chores such as stretching canvas and keeping the shop clean. Chances are slim that you will actually work on paintings during this period. But after you get a feel for the work you can apply to an institute that teaches art restoration on the graduate level. Here are three:

University of Delaware
Winterthur Museum
Winterthur, DE 19735

Institute of Fine Arts
14 East 78th Street
New York, NY 10021

Cooperstown Graduate Program in Conservation
Cooperstown, NY 13326

These institutes train students by having them work on samples first, then letting them do restoration under strict supervision, and finally letting them in professional internships. Upon reaching a level of professional competence, art restorers earn between $16,000 and $30,000 when working for museums. The fees charged by private restorers vary with their reputation.

A distinct downside of the profession is its reliance on chemicals, some of which may be toxic. Art restorers have to be very aware of the need for laboratory safety procedures. Restoration is not a profession for people with large artistic egos. No points for trying to "out-Rembrandt Rembrandt." There is, however, the distinct satisfaction of being in close communion with art and artists, and knowing that your efforts will help to preserve something of beauty for future generations.

7 Astrologer

Astrologers do more than simply wish upon a star. Using a person's exact birth time and location, they chart the energy patterns that will affect that person through the course of life.

A specific chart for an individual is a very precise calculation that is far removed from the generalized horoscopes that appear in daily newspapers. Computers are revolutionizing the profession by bringing a far greater degree of accuracy to the plotting of planetary positions and transits that are an astrologer's reference points.

Linda Hill of New York City, who has been an astrologer for 17 years, says that people usually seek a consultation when there are events in their life that mystify them. By using a person's birth (natal) chart and progressed chart (which indicates where planets currently are located), an astrologer can help put events in perspective by giving them an overview as to their circumstances in life and how they can be used for personal growth. Hill said that a chart is useful in predicting events over a three-month period, adding that what keeps clients coming back are the accuracies of predictions.

To be accurate, a prospective astrologer should first take courses in the field and then follow through with lifelong study, experimentation, and reading. One center that offers a three-year course of study is the:

New York Astrology Center
63 West 38th Street
New York, NY 10018

Students cover such areas as chart interpretation, astronomy, computers and astrology, systems of astrology, and the history of the discipline. Another source of information about workshops and centers is the:

American Federation of Astrologers
P.O. Box 22040
Tempe, AZ 85282

The study of astrology is very rigorous since it requires the mastery of a whole new vocabulary, and an understanding of much technical data. Astrologers must then use this knowledge to augment their intuitive ability. Hill described astrology as a profession that integrates the functions of both the left and right sides of the brain.

A consultation lasts about 90 minutes, and an astrologer usually devotes an equal amount of time to preparation. Fees range between $50 and $150 depending upon the area of the country and on an individual's reputation. There is also the possibility of becoming an astrology writer, as more publications are featuring a regular astrology column for their readers.

One of the main attractions of astrology is that it never gets boring. "The problems and people are always different," Hill said. "I have the opportunity to contribute to a person's life in a profound way."

8 Astronaut

The deaths of the astronauts aboard the Challenger spacecraft brought home to people the sobering fact that space travel is dangerous. But this still did not dissuade Americans from applying to become astronauts. Indeed, for the training classes of 1987, over 1,500 people applied (out of which 17 were chosen). As long as space is the final frontier it will attract men and women who have the spirit of adventure.

Astronauts come from both military and civilian backgrounds. Pilots are picked exclusively from a pool of high-performance jet pilots with over 1,000 hours of flight time. Civilian mission specialists are men and women who have advanced training in academic disciplines such as mathematics, astronomy and the physical sciences, or biology and medicine. To qualify, you must be between five feet and six feet in height, with eyesight corrected to 20/20 in each eye.

Steve Nesbitt of the Johnson Space Center in Houston said recruitment is an ongoing process and an application can be obtained by writing to

Duayne Ross
Astronaut Selection Office
AH611
Johnson Space Center
Houston, TX 77058

In addition to having the proper academic background, Nesbitt said, astronauts must be willing to commit to a long-term goal, should enjoy people, and display a willingness to adapt to new tasks. "We've had doctors who wound up tinkering on satellites," Nesbitt said.

Astronauts earn between $35,000 and $45,000 per year and are with the program an average of 10 years. During training an astronaut takes further courses in fields such as computers, guidance and navigation, and astronomy and meteorology. Time is spent in weightless simulation drills and in learning to function in a space suit.

Once a crew of astronauts is assigned to a specific flight, they are cross-trained so that every crew member can handle the duties of at least one other associate. Further briefings are held on spacecraft systems and payload requirements, and astronauts spend long hours in flight simulation. Training reaches its peak several weeks before the flight when flight crew and ground controllers practice the entire mission in a joint training exercise. Hopefully, during the actual flight there will be no hidden surprises. But no matter how well prepared they are, the wonders of space will still evoke awe from the men and women of earth.

9 Auctioneer

An auction is as close as one gets to the "perfect marketplace" envisioned by classical economists. As a way of determining the real value of goods, it is a tough method to beat. Besides, it is exciting when the bidding gets spirited and hands fly up all over the auction arena. At the apex of this supply and demand curve stands the auctioneer, the "colonel" (a traditional honorary title), who maintains the crowd's interest by rhythmically chanting to draw out the optimum bid.

Auctioneers are showmen (or showwomen) with a keen business acumen. Their job involves the preparation and actual sale of merchandise, which could be almost anything, including household furnishings, automobiles, livestock, art, antiques, foodstuffs such as produce and coffee, raw materials, surplus government equipment, and real estate. Before an auction occurs, an auctioneer sees to it that necessary permits are obtained and that merchandise is properly catalogued and advertised. Contracts are signed with the seller concerning percentages of commission and goods are displayed in a way that is attractive to the public. Once the auction starts, the auctioneer and his assistants, called "ringmen," keep a close watch for fresh bids and generate enthusiasm through a crowd psychology that consists of joking and cajoling the bidders. A good auctioneer's chant is pleasing to the ear. At the same time it informs the public about the highest bid that has been received.

You do not need the lungs of an opera singer to maintain an auctioneer's chant for hours on end. The techniques of breathing can be learned from a practicing auctioneer or by attending an auction school. A listing of schools can be obtained from trade papers put out by the:

National Auctioneer Association
8880 Ballentine Street
Overland Park, KS 66214

Once you have the basics, there are several ways to begin a career. The first involves working with an established firm as a ringman or assistant auctioneer. This allows you to develop confidence and professional experience. For those interested in striking out on their own, it is important to develop exposure. This is usually done by volunteering your services as an auctioneer for a charitable function. Business increases as your abilities become recognized, some auctioneers eventually choose to specialize in one particular field.

An auctioneer is paid a percentage of the gross receipts of a sale. The income potential is virtually unlimited, and the start-up investment is minimal, making this business even more attractive. Auctioneering once again shows that a person does not need to be a captain of industry to be a colonel of capitalism.

10 Band Roadie

A concert tour puts the roll in a rock 'n roll band's performances. In a circuit that can stretch from around the local beer joints to around the world, bands have a tradition of taking to the road to bring music and good times to their faithful followers. Accompanying them as sherpas on these rock expeditions are the band roadies.

The term roadie has come to mean the entire entourage that stages a concert. This includes sound and light technicians, band technicians, tour managers, stage managers, and other support personnel such as bus drivers and accountants. For a band that is on a nationwide tour, the typical crew has between 15 and 40 people.

To be successful as a roadie, you must be willing to give up a regular sleep cycle. A normal day for a traveling band involves arriving at a concert hall at 9 a.m., having a catered breakfast, doing lights at 10 a.m., dinner at 6 p.m., show at 8 p.m., taking down the equipment at 1 a.m., and then getting back into the bus to sleep until the next town. As Pete Heffernen, who was a roadie for six years, put it, "You never get a chance to see what Terre Haute looks like." Since a band usually performs five nights a week, a roadie's life can be tiring. Yet, for many there is an urge to heed Willie Nelson's call of being "on the road again." A tight-knit camaraderie develops among roadies and there are other benefits of the music world that make the travel enjoyable.

Heffernen said there are many ways to break into the business and most involve being at the right place at the right time. You can start by working with a local bar band and then expanding your contacts and gaining experience. Familiarity with electrical and sound components is a definite plus, along with physical strength to move around speakers, light stands, and other large equipment. Other roadies have gotten a start when they were hired to replace an original crew member who was fired or had to leave the tour. Word of mouth is a major factor, and Heffernen said that once a person starts traveling and becomes immersed in the business, personal reference is the key to information about job openings.

A roadie will usually start by moving equipment and then graduate to installing and securing lights and sound panels. The salary range depends on the popularity of the band, the skill of the roadie, and the length of the tour, but it ranges between $500 and $1,500 per week. This is a freelance job, and it goes without saying that roadies must enjoy traveling. They cannot be planted in some city like granite, but should instead resemble rolling stones.

11 Baseball Umpire

Just like the captain of a ship, the baseball umpire is absolute master of his or her domain. An ump's word is law, not subject to appeal, and glacial calm in the face of screaming managers is the stuff from which baseball legends are made.

Yes, the umpire is the master of the baseball diamond and, as one might suspect, the end product of a very demanding training and apprenticeship program. Umpires must be high school graduates with good eyesight and common sense. They need not be athletes and need never have had prior umpiring experience. However, they must take a six-week course at one of these schools to be considered for the program:

Joe Brinkman Umpire School
P.O. Box 40308
St. Petersburg, FL 33743

Harry Wendelstadt Umpire School
88 South St. Andrews Drive
Ormond Beach, FL 32074

New York School of Umpiring, Inc.
P.O.Box 1226
Riverdale, NY 10471

Each of these schools selects its top 12 candidates who then go on to Bradenton, Florida, for another one-week training session. At this point, representatives of the two major leagues and the Office for Baseball Umpire Development (201 Bayshore Drive SE, St. Petersburg,

FL 33731) select individuals for minor league positions that come open. If there are not enough minor league slots to accommodate everyone, those not selected must go through the whole process again the next year.

Once you are in the system, you must display hustle, common sense, and strong leadership abilities to continue progressing up the career ladder. Umpires earn $1,600 per month in Class A minor league ball, and it usually takes eight years in the minors before an umpire becomes eligible for a major league diamond.

The Baseball Umpire Development Program holds high standards for its recruits. "The successful umpire," it says in its guide to umpiring, "must be even-tempered but mentally strong enough to handle situations under stress conditions. He must have the physical and mental strength to take charge of any unusual situation that might arise. He must have a keen desire to improve as an umpire at all times, he must be able to accept constructive criticism and he must be able to learn from his mistakes."

The guide goes on to suggest that umpires should also have a knowledge of management skills, sociology, Spanish, and English grammar and speech. It does not, however, suggest that you take the latter two so seriously that you would object to the pronunciation of "Steerike One."

12 Baton Teacher

What goes up must come down.

Well, okay, that is true. But the spangled majorettes and high-stepping drum majors help to make the going up and coming down of a glittering baton a classy production. Assisting them in developing their skill and showmanship are professional baton teachers.

Baton teachers are usually women who were avid twirlers in their youth, at which time they mastered the skills they now teach to others. Baton teacher M.J. Long of Waterford, New York, said that a teacher should know at least the following basic moves of twirling: flat twirls, side twirls, figure eights, ferris wheels, around the world, spins, and finger twirls. A teacher should also know the basics of choreography in order to help her students go through their routines and work up new ones.

Mrs. Long also recommended that prospective teachers affiliate themselves with the National Baton Twirling Association. The address is:

National Baton Twirling Association
P.O. Box 266
Janesville, WI 53547-0266

The association sponsors regional and national competitions. One way for a teacher to hone her skills is to sit as a scoring judge at these competitions.

As for teaching, Mrs. Long said there are several routes to take. One is to contact a local department of recreation and try to negotiate a contract with them. A second is to teach twirling routines to high school majorettes through a contract with a local school district. A third method is to open a studio of your own or to offer your services through an existing dance studio.

As for tuitions, Mrs. Long said ballpark figures are $2 to $3 per student per class for simple twirling instruction at recreation departments, and $20 to $45 per hour of individual instruction for students entering major competitions. Most baton teachers use their talents as a way of generating a fun second income.

If you are dedicated, talented, and qualified, you should have no trouble in twirling your students around your little finger.

13 Blacksmith

Smithing is one of mankind's oldest industrial crafts. A reference in Genesis mentions "Tubal Cain, an instructor of every artificer in brass and iron." The ancient Romans believed that the volcano Vesuvius was the home of Vulcan, the god of metalworking. In fact, smiths have always used spark-spewing forges to work iron into a variety of useful shapes.

The village smithy has taken on a big-city status in recent years, as blacksmiths are now being called upon to add decorative touches to ironwork door grills and window guards. Modern-day smiths still use time-honored tools such as anvils, hammers, and tongs in their endeavors, but they also have a modern understanding of metal stress, design, mechanics, engineering, and accounting. A blacksmith is a natural "fixer" who enjoys working with his hands as well as his head.

Blacksmithing is often combined with the trade of welding, and there are trade school and college-level courses available in both. A list of schools that offer such instruction can be obtained from the:

**National Blacksmith and Welders
Association (NBWA)**
c/o James Holman
P.O. Box 327
Arnold, NE 69120

Some smiths learn their trade through apprenticeships and self-study. The NBWA has a membership list that can assist you in finding a master smith. As for books on blacksmithing and necessary supplies, an excellent source is the:

Centaur Forge Ltd.
P.O. Box 340V
Burlington, WI 53105

Useful current books on the subject include *The Practical Handbook of Blacksmithing and Metalworking* by Percy W. Blandford, and *The Blacksmith's Source Book: An Annotated Bibliography* by James E. Fleming.

There are certain hazards associated with the craft. Molten metal can cause nasty burns, and fumes must be well vented to prevent respiratory diseases. Smiths are willing to risk such drawbacks to enjoy the challenge of working with metal. Nearly 60 percent of the shops employ no more than three people. Experienced smiths earn from $15,000 to $25,000, depending on locale. The type of work varies depending on whether the shop is located in a rural or urban area. Rural shops deal in repairs to farm equipment and fabrication of one-of-a-kind parts. Urban smiths, in addition to creating grillwork, create items such as designer fireplace tongs and pokers. In fact, it has been said that the only things a blacksmith cannot do is repair the crack of dawn or mend a broken heart.

14 Braille Word Processor

Braille word processors have a sharp eye and a soft touch. They need these skills because they must deal with texts appearing in both written form and in braille.

Word processors take books and magazines, key in the words, and create a finished copy in braille instead of printed text. Sounds simple enough, but when the corrections come back from the proofreaders, the word processor then reads the dots by sight and then makes the changes. This skill in braille reading takes several months to learn and is taught on the job, according to Diane Croft, marketing manager of the National Braille Press.

"The word processing skills are the same, but people come to work here when they are bored out of their skulls working for a bank or law firm. People experience a sense of mission here that they don't get elsewhere," she said. For their efforts, braille word processors earn between $15 and $22 per hour.

For a person considering such a parallel job shift, there are five firms that specialize in braille publishing. They are:

American Printing House for the Blind
1839 Frankfort Avenue
Louisville, KY 40206

Associated Services for the Blind
919 Walnut Street
Philadelphia, PA 19107

National Braille Press
88 St. Stephen Street
Boston, MA 02115

Transformation Inc.
3132 SE J Street
Stuart, FL 33494

15 Brewmeister

Excavations of Egyptian archaeological sites and translations of hieroglyphic temple tablets have conclusively proven that these ancient people knew about both beer making and beer consuming. The only question that has not been determined is whether they preferred bottles or cans.

Indeed, some scholars believe that mankind has been brewing beer since the dawn of the agricultural age. Amazingly enough, the basic recipe really has not changed, but then the finer things in life never do. Considering this unbroken historical record, being a brewmeister can thus be considered the world's third oldest profession. Modern-day brewers, however, are a bit more technical than their ancient counterparts were. A strong college background in chemistry, math, and physics is suggested for those considering brewing as a career.

A brewmeister is the person who makes sure that every six-pack of beer produced by a brewery adheres to the company recipe. The chief brewmeister and his assistants preside over all phases of the beer-making process. This usually involves analyzing, on a daily basis, the corn, malt, hops, and water that are used. As the beer goes through various fermentation states, carbon dioxide levels are checked, specific gravity is tested, and color noted. Since the raw materials are variable (a batch of hops might have suffered from drought, for instance), the brewmeister must be highly skilled to produce a consistent product.

This skill comes by learning the profession starting at the bottom of a fermentation tank. Jake Leinenkugel, head of Leinenkugel Brewery in Chippewa Falls, Wisconsin, suggested that a person interested in the field apply to a brewery whose beer they enjoy. Addresses can be found on the side of the can or via the *Modern Brewery Age Blue Book*, which can be found in a reference library.

The love of the product is essential, since prospective brewmeisters will spend anywhere from several months to several years scrubbing and sterilizing fermentation tanks. After this initiation into the profession, if the desire is still there and if you have the necessary educational background, a brewmeister may then recommend to the company that you receive advanced training at the:

Seibel Institute of Technology
4049 West Peterson Avenue
Chicago, IL 60646

The Institute is renowned for its beer-making curriculum and it graduated many of the brewmeisters working today.

Leinenkugel noted that a brewmeister must be conscientious and attentive to detail. Decisions that are made in the brewing room determine a company's standing in the barroom. Salary is commensurate with responsibility. A brewmeister can earn between $25,000 and $75,000 yearly depending on geographic location and company size. If you view the odor of fermentation as the sweet smell of success, then a brewmeister's life may be one to which to say "Cheers!"

16 Bridal Consultant

What does a bridal consultant do? Well, it's simple. She takes care of all the wedding details except getting the groom to say "I do."

That little nutshell explanation doesn't do justice to the intricate planning that goes into the successful staging of a wedding. Hundreds of details must be attended to, details such as cake design, gown style, and flower placement. Faced with so many choices on her own, a young bride may panic and elope.

"Today, most of the traditional wedding planners (such as mothers, aunts, and older sisters) are working. They don't have the time to do all of the legwork, so they are turning to people who can recommend good choices to them," said Gerard Monaghan, president of the Association of Bridal Consultants.

Monaghan said that bridal consultants usually enter the profession in one of two ways. Either they help family members or friends with their weddings and discover they enjoy making people happy, or they enter through a wedding-related business such as catering or the floral trade.

There is no formal training program for consultants but the trade association supplies a home study course to help you improve your professional skill. The course can be obtained from the:

Association of Bridal Consultants
200 Chestnutland Road
New Milford, CT 06776-2521

In addition, Monaghan said, it is helpful for a person to take college-level courses in psychology, business, sociology, and food service management.

The most important asset of a bridal consultant is her "black book" of reputable businesses and entertainers that cater to the bridal trade. Typically, a bride-to-be will tell a consultant her wedding budget, and the consultant then recommends services in that range.

Monaghan said it is customary for the consultant to charge 15 percent of the gross cost of the wedding, although some consultants work on a flat fee, on an hourly basis, or on rebates from suppliers. A bridal consultant's yearly salary depends on the number of bookings. Some consultants are so busy, they may also employ the services of freelance consultants to handle overloads of work. Fortunately for consultants, brides are spreading their weddings more evenly throughout the calendar, so they don't run into a situation of an overloaded June and slack months the rest of the year.

Those people who do best in the profession know the needs of a bride, have exemplary organizational skills, and possess a keen eye for details. When the organist plays "The Wedding March" the consultant can relax—the job is done. The bride's job is just beginning.

17 Busker

Busking is the fine art of entertaining people on street corners. Magicians, jugglers, fire-eaters, contortionists, acrobats, mimes, musicians, in short, those performers who refused to expire when vaudeville died, all belong to this guild. And a guild it is, since many buskers know each other from wandering a circuit that takes them around the United States and the world.

To be successful, a busker needs an eye-catching gimmick to get people to stop, and a definable act. The first is important since people are not buying tickets to the performance and need an incentive to stay and watch. The second convinces people that yes, they have been entertained, and it was well worth it. Talent is also helpful, but verve and showmanship reign supreme when it comes to street theatre. One busker had as his act "Fluffy the Wonder Dog," which featured a mongrel basset hound that sat on the sidewalk while its owner extolled the difficult tricks Fluffy could not perform. People cheerfully kicked into the passed hat when the busker announced the money would be used as a scholarship fund for Fluffy.

Performers who do well at busking are those folks who simply must entertain others. It's in their blood, and busking provides an outlet for acts that would not otherwise have a commercial market in today's entertainment world. It has the advantage of being immediately accessible. Once a busker feels that he or she is ready, the stage is right around the corner. As might be guessed, however, a premium is placed on those areas that have a constant flow of pedestrian traffic. Weather also affects performers. The show must go on, but it can wait until after a rainstorm is over.

Cities vary in their acceptance of buskers. San Francisco, Seattle, Madison, and New York all have active groups of buskers, but the spiritual center of the tradition is in Key West, Florida, which holds an international busker festival in January of each year. Anyone interested in the profession should attend, since it is a great opportunity to sharpen skills and exchange information. No formal academy exists to train buskers. Each person develops his or her talent in an individual manner. Earnings can vary from a few quarters to over $200 for an evening's work. As one busker put it, "Folks, applause to me is like butter. What I need is bread." And he got it.

18 Cartographer

Mapmaking seems to be one of those skills that have faded out with time. After all, most folks are fairly certain that the earth is round, the Rocky Mountains are somewhere out West, the Bronx is up and the Battery is down. But today's mapmakers do much more than illustrate empty areas of the globe. Weather maps, hiking trail maps, street maps, navigational maps, world events maps, textbook maps, and scores of other specialty maps are needed by people to precisely pinpoint locations.

To satisfy this demand, there are over 60 universities that offer courses of study in cartography. A complete list of these schools, along with an informative career brochure, can be obtained from the:

**American Congress of Surveying and
   Mapping**
210 Little Falls Street
Falls Church, VA 22046

California cartographer Patricia Caldwell Lindgren said that modern-day mapmakers still draw maps by hand for some projects, using aerial photos to provide information on terrain and relative locations. Increasingly, however, cartographers utilize the design and graphic capabilities supplied by computers to make their task easier. Artistic talents and knowledge of computers are both useful, and it is important for a mapmaker to have a good spatial sense.

Ms. Caldwell said cartographers usually start their career with the federal government, working for departments such as the Defense Mapping Agency or the National Geodetic Survey. Federal employment alone accounts for up to 50 percent of all cartographers. The remainder work for state and local governments, private firms such as the American Automobile Association, or as consultants. Incomes range from $20,000 to $60,000 with the larger salaries paid to those professionals who can also correctly fold maps.

19 Chimney Sweep

The chimney sweep has one foot placed in the top-hatted lore of yesteryear and the other planted in modern methods of preventing hazardous chimney fires that are the by-product of wood and coal burning.

There are many quaint stories surrounding the profession. One is that the tradition of top hat and tails was originated by sweeps who appropriated worn-out garments discarded by undertakers. Another is that a bristle from a sweep's broom is supposed to bring good luck during the coming year. The romance of the profession has thus attracted certain mavericks who do not enjoy a buttoned-down daily routine. This spirit of entrepreneurism has given rise to a number of owner-operated companies run by individuals or partners. In any case, most sweeps will agree that the dust and dirt involved with the profession hardly make it worthwhile to work for somebody else.

Chimney sweeping involves removal of the flammable substance called creosote from the inside walls of a chimney. Creosote forms when smoke particles prematurely cool and condense on the chimney interior as they rise up the flue. This creosote builds up layers on the inside of the chimney, and can ignite. The resulting fire could burn down a house.

Sweeps attack the creosote problem by brushing the inside of the flue with steel-bristled brushes attached to flexible fiberglass rods. For wood stoves, sweeps climb to the top of a roof, lean over the chimney and shove the brushes down the flue. The resulting debris is then gathered from a trap door at the bottom of the chimney and carted away.

When sweeping fireplaces, a sweep hunches inside the fireplace and pushes the brush up the chimney. The flexible rod allows the sweep to bend around the obstructions within the fireplace. As might be guessed, the creosote falls on the sweep during this process. High-powered vacuums are used to control the resulting cloud of dust and a sweep uses a respirator and goggles as personal protection.

Although the basic process is straightforward, there are many nuances involved and novices usually find it worthwhile to apprentice with an existing sweep or to attend one of the chimney sweep schools listed with the:

National Chimney Sweep Guild
P.O. Box 1078
Merrimac, NH 03054

This profession involves more than going to work in the morning and then collecting a paycheck. Men and women who are sweeps are independent business-people who must attend to bookkeeping and marketing in addition to sweeping chimneys. In this respect, a sweep must wear many hats in addition to a top hat.

If you live in a region where wood burning is popular, it might be worthwhile to weigh the several-thousand-dollar capital outlay needed to start a business against the rising demand for sweep services. Depending on the area of the country, a sweep charges between $30 and $75 to clean a chimney. It is possible to clean five to eight chimneys per day. Most of the work is done in the fall and spring since a wood-burning chimney should be swept on a yearly basis. There is also a potential to develop a related retail business with such products as stovepipes and chimney caps, and fireplace inserts. Some sweeps are branching into chimney repair by tuck-pointing old brick or installing new chimney liners. The National Guild conducts seminars on such subjects at its annual convention and runs a certification program to promote professional competence.

This is a dirty profession, no doubt about it. Roofs may prove hazardous and old mortar may crumble at the touch, bringing down an avalanche of bricks. But there is a charm to a profession whose members outfit themselves in top hat and tails to go to work. The only other folks who are so attired are diplomats and kings, and they are not nearly as lucky.

20 Chocolatier

The good news is that the stuff tastes great.

The bad news is that this is a profession where it is very, very easy to put on weight. If you are obsessed with following every new onion and prune juice diet that hits the tabloids, turn to the next section.

To the American public, chocolate is more than just a candy. It has become a lifestyle. This is good news for America's chocolate manufacturers, and, in turn, for the chocolatiers who oversee the creation of the consumable delights.

There are several branches of the industry with which a person can become involved. The primary phase is the manufacture of the chocolate, which involves grinding cocoa beans and combining them with sugar, milk, and cocoa butter.

As in beer making, the quality and consistency of the raw materials vary, so a chocolatier must be part good cook, part chemist, and part connoisseur to insure a consistent product. Malcolm Campbell of the Van Leer Chocolate Corporation, Jersey City, New Jersey, said a good sense of taste is absolutely essential, since taste is the way good cocoa beans are distinguished from bad ones. Campbell noted that experience as a cook or dietician is very helpful, since a chocolatier will always be weighing or measuring ingredients.

Another way to enter the profession is by studying confectionery practices at schools offering degrees in food sciences, such as Pennsylvania State University and Cornell University. Or you can seek employment with a chocolate company. Find its address through its product label or by contacting the:

Chocolate Manufacturing Association
7900 Westpark Drive, Suite 514
McLean, VA 22102

Beginning chocolatiers average about $12,000 per year as lab assistants and can progress up to $65,000 per year as lab directors. The lab is the heart of the chocolate operation, for it is here where raw materials are tested and the final product sampled. Much of this work involves on-the-job training, and afterwards a person with sufficient aptitude can progress to the research and development field.

It is also possible to work for companies or small stores that make confections of their own flavor and design. If this retail aspect sounds appealing, you can work at a specialty shop to gain direct experience making such favorites as chocolate bunny rabbits.

Being a chocolatier is definitely a profession into which you can sink a sweet tooth. The key to success, however, is to grow in experience instead of girth.

21 Clown

How many teachers are there who wish they could send their class clown to a class for clowns?

They really need look no further. At the Florida winter home of The Greatest Show On Earth, the Ringling Brothers and Barnum & Bailey Circus operates the world's only Clown College. Those individuals who have an abiding desire to clown around can study such challenging disciplines as pie-throwing and squirting seltzer water down someone's pants.

To find out about the school, write to

Ringling Brothers and Barnum & Bailey
Clown College
Director of Admissions
3201 New Mexico Avenue, NW
Washington, DC 20016

Getting admitted to the school, however, is not as easy as sliding on a banana peel. Applicants must be at least 17 years of age. Although no prior clowning experience is necessary, they must complete and send to the school what is certainly academia's most creative admission application. Forget about SAT scores and calculus grades. This application asks questions such as, "List five movies you'd like to see again," or "When was the last time you cried and for what reason?" These questions are meant to get to a person's soul instead of merely the cerebellum.

Each year's class admits 60 students to the 10 1/2-

week program. Although tuition is free, students must pay for their own room and board during this period. Classes are taught by over two dozen professional performers and provide a thorough exposure to a clown's craft. The most important assets you can bring to the school are the desire to be a good clown and a willingness to devote yourself to the profession.

Students create their own routines and experiment in the makeup room to discover their greasepaint personality. They also learn such skills as juggling, walking on wires, riding a unicycle, slapstick, mime, walking on stilts, choreography, and improvisation. Constant attention is paid to honing comic timing and observing safety techniques.

Graduation consists of a gala performance in which everyone participates. However, after commencement there will be tears for some clowns since only an average of 20 are hired to become part of the traveling road show. Ringling clowns go through a further three years of coaching and training before they can be considered master clowns. Those who do not become part of the circus have the tools to become quite successful performers at children's parties and on television shows in their hometowns.

A clown's life can be a grueling one and is not especially lucrative. The Ringling Brothers Circus spends 11 months of the year on the road, during which time the performers sleep on the train. Circus clowns average about $200 per week, out of which they must pay for meals and a monthly $40 charge to stay on the train. The constant travel is the main reason that clowns leave the circus. But as one staff member said, "If you love the work, the work will love you. Money can't buy the satisfaction you get. If you're good, you can spend a lifetime making people happy."

22 College Basketball Referee

A zebra is a blind, deaf critter who is always looking in the wrong direction. Nevertheless, on a college basketball court, a zebra/referee is king of the jungle.

College basketball referees actually do have good eyesight, and their only physical peculiarity is that they are a bit thick-skinned. The referees for both men's and women's basketball are the products of an on-the-job training program that begins in the sweaty gyms of junior high schools across the land.

Referees must have good eyesight and be in healthy physical condition. To become a National Collegiate Athletic Association (NCAA) basketball ref, you should first contact the:

National Federation of State High School Associations
11724 Plaza Circle
P.O. Box 20626
Kansas City, MO 64195

The federation will provide the address of your state association.

You start by passing the state's certifying exam on rules. Then you begin working your way up through the ranks–junior high games, junior varsity games, and finally high school ball. All the while you attend clinics and seminars to improve your skills. After about five years on the high school level, you can send an application to the college conference in your area. If your skill and confidence are exemplary, the conference referee assigner may then start working you into their games.

Hank Nichols, who is the NCAA national coordinator of men's officiating, said that people from all walks of life double as referees, "We have doctors, lawyers, firemen, teachers, policemen, businessmen, you name it." For their services, NCAA referees receive between $175 and $350 per game, depending on the conference. Nichols said that referees fit their basketball games around their existing work schedules. "Travel can be tough. A person needs flexibility if he wants to work games outside of his conference," he noted.

Referees take to the court for many reasons. For some it's a challenge, for others, it's a love of the game. Although fans may rant and rave to the contrary, refs really try to keep their decisions impartial. "We go out there to do a job. Each game will have a loser and a winner, and we try to give both teams a chance," Nichols said.

23 Congressional Page

One of the best ways for young people to become involved with the national political process is to become a congressional page. Pages are young men and women in their eleventh year of school who serve the members of the House of Representatives and Senate when these bodies are in session.

Pages are appointed by the nation's senators and congressmen, so if you are interested, the first thing to do is to write a letter to your representative requesting an appointment. A local post office is an excellent place to get the address of your representative. In your letter you should explain why you want to become a page. Pages are selected on the basis of scholastic achievement and activity in school and community affairs. Letters of recommendation attesting to character will also be required.

Upon appointment, pages attend school from 6:10 a.m. to 10:30 a.m. (There are two 18-week semesters, one from September to January, and another from February to June.) After class is dismissed, the pages report to the House and Senate where they distribute the day's bills and resolutions and act as messengers for the legislators. Sometimes pages work past midnight during lengthy debates. A page must be absolutely trustworthy and must have the stamina to deal with long hours.

While in Washington, a page lives at a residence hall on Capitol Hill and is billed $300 per month for a room and evening meals. Page salaries are $757 per month or $9,090 per year. The experiences that a page gains can prove invaluable. Many use their training to get further involved in the political process and several have been elected to office in their own right.

There are further opportunities on the state level to become either legislative pages or sergeants-at-arms (they both have essentially the same duties). The various states have different methods of choosing these individuals. Connecticut, for instance, uses only senior citizens. New Jersey uses both senior citizens and students, and West Virginia has a "page for a day" system in which students come to the state capitol to serve for one day during the term. Salary rates vary, and these posts are usually controlled by state legislators as patronage positions. Active participation in local politics is often needed to gain these appointments. Contact your state senator or representative.

24 Croupier

Winners may come and go but the house always plays the game. In the two gambling oases of America—Atlantic City and Las Vegas—tens of thousands of convention-goers and gamblers spend their moola trying to win the favor of the fickle goddess of chance. Always ready to accommodate them with a turn of the card or a roll of the dice are the croupiers.

Other than bank tellers there are few workers whose job involves handling so much money. Consequently, there is a great deal of attention paid to making sure the game is played right. Atlantic City and Nevada differ in the training of their respective work forces, but in either case, being a croupier calls for a pleasant attitude that allows both winners and losers to have a good time.

In Las Vegas, croupiers only need to prove proficiency. They can thus come in "off the street" or learn at one of the schools located in Las Vegas. In Atlantic City, beginners must first attend state-approved schools that teach gambling procedures. Two schools are:

Casino Schools, Inc.
1823 Bacharach Boulevard
Atlantic City, NJ 08401

**Atlantic Community College Casino Career
    Institute**
1535 Bacharach Boulevard
Atlantic City, NJ 08401

At these schools, students must learn the rules and procedures of a "primary" and a "secondary" game. Blackjack and craps are primary games and they involve between 160 and 240 hours of classroom training. Secondary games such as roulette and baccarat require 80 to 120 hours of training. In addition to spending time developing a smooth dealer technique, students learn skills such as handling drunks and compulsive gamblers. Once the course is successfully completed, a croupier completes a 22-page application for the New Jersey Casino Control Commission. Backgrounds are checked and anyone convicted of a felony is automatically rejected. Once approved by the state a person should have little trouble getting a job, according to Peter Demos, president of Casino Schools.

Dealers work a nine- to ten-hour shift with a 20-minute break each hour. They run the games and, in turn, answer to a hierarchy consisting of a floor person, a pit boss, a shift boss, and the casino manager. These latter folks oversee the tables and dispense such "perks" as show tickets to high-rollers.

Demos said dealers earn between $24,000 and $32,000 per year including tips. Despite the substantial salary there is still a 20 percent annual turnover in the industry. The relatively young ages of the dealers, sensitivity to cigarette smoke, the constant jangling of slot machines, and boredom all take their toll.

But just as a casino is always eager to welcome back its high-rollers, it is happy to welcome back croupiers who remain in good standing with the Gaming Commission. Demos said this aspect of flexibility makes casino work an attractive career prospect. In addition, summer help is always needed in both Las Vegas and Atlantic City.

Prospective croupiers should visit a casino and talk to several of the dealers during their break. This is a good way to find out if this career gamble is a good bet for you.

25 Cruise Ship Entertainer

Cruise ship entertainers provide high fun on the high seas. Their acts help to shape the general mood of enjoyment aboard the ship–which is fine, so long as audiences do not go overboard with enthusiasm.

Singers, magicians, comedians, novelty acts, and revue companies are all needed to perform for periods of one week to three months. The prime agency that books shows for cruise lines is the:

Bramson Entertainment Agency
1440 Broadway
New York, NY 10018

Bramson is looking for individuals with established routines, since a boat is not the place to break in a new act. They are interested in entertainers who perform for night clubs and conventions. Salaries vary according to the act. Entertainers seeking to do the cruise ship circuit should write (do not call) the agency requesting an audition. In lieu of auditions, the agency also accepts videotapes of performances.

The style of entertainment and the schedule will vary with each cruise line. While on board, the performers stay in a staff cabin and when not on stage they mingle with passengers as good-will public relation representatives. The chance to travel overseas while getting paid to do it are enticements for this job.

If an American seeks a staff position as a cook, nurse, steward, or deckhand on a cruise ship, then the

51

procedure is to apply to firms that travel intracoastal runs between American ports. You should have experience in the job for which you are applying and membership in a maritime union may be necessary.

Here are three cruise lines that visit American ports:

Clipper Cruise Line
7711 Bonhomme Street
St. Louis, MO 63105

American Cruise Lines
1 Marine Park
Haddam, CT 06438

American Hawaii Cruises
604 Fort Street
Honolulu, HA 96813

The suggested employment route is to write to the personnel director of these companies to inquire about salary schedules and openings.

26 Film Extra

Movie extras will be the first to agree, "They don't make them like they used to." The salad days of the profession occurred when films featured "casts of thousands." But there is still a demand for men and women to fill the open spaces of modern day television or movie sets.

To pursue the profession of being a movie extra, you should live near Los Angeles or New York City, as these cities are the twin hubs of the film and television industry. In California, you must present to the Screen Extra's Guild a contract from a casting agency such as Disc or Central (two of the major ones, both located in Burbank) certifying they are representing you. The Guild is located at the:

Screen Extra's Guild
3629 Cahuenga Boulevard West
Los Angeles, CA 90068

You are required to pay a one-time $655 initiation fee, a figure that drops to $55 biannually in succeeding years. Extra actor Will West explained that after you become a Guild member, you can work as an extra on television and movie sets within a 300-mile radius of Los Angeles.

Studios notify the casting agencies of their needs, be it for women, black actors, older or younger actors, etc. Extras call the casting agencies, usually between 10 a.m. and 6 p.m. to see if there would be any work for them the following day. West said it is helpful for an extra to have a wardrobe composed of several modern suits or dresses, Western wear, "seedy" clothes, work clothes, and formal wear. Anything of a period or specialized nature would be supplied by the production company's wardrobe department. When on the set, extras follow the director's instructions, working anywhere from 1 to 12 hours per day. Based on an 8-hour day, a union extra earns $90 per day.

In New York, extra work is controlled by the Screen Actors Guild. The Guild is located at the:

Screen Actors Guild
1700 Broadway
New York, NY 10019

To become a member, a person must present to the Guild a contract showing they have at least one or two speaking lines in a movie. The Guild then grants a waiver to the person to work in the film after which it requires an initiation fee of $800.50 for further work. This figure lowers to twice yearly dues of $42.50 and 1.5 percent of all yearly earnings over $5,000. Another way to become a member is to belong to a related union such as Actor's Equity (stage shows) or AFTRA, the union that covers television and radio work.

As for why people seek to become extras, the answer is easy–they want to be in movies. "Extras just love working around movies, and there is always the hope that a director will spot their talents," West said. When they aren't working on sets, extras supplement their income with part-time jobs such as chauffeuring or restaurant work. The stories of starving actors are not all true, but some are. Any type of film work requires a lot of dedication for not much recompense. It requires a person who truly seeks the stars.

27 Fire Tower Lookout

"They also serve who sit and watch" can be called the motto of several hundred fire tower lookouts with the U.S. Forest Service. If you are gregarious and like bright lights, forget this job. Fire towers are usually in the proverbial middle of nowhere, and the long hours of solitude are punctuated only by fire check calls and visits from occasional hikers. But if time spent surrounded by the beauty of nature sounds appealing, then a fire tower job can provide a bird's eye view of God's green earth.

Fire tower lookouts and aerial observers are key links in the Forest Service's efforts to control forest fires in its vast holdings, which are located primarily in states west of the Mississippi. Sitting high on a mountaintop, the lookout scans the horizon for unusual signs of smoke. If smoke is spotted, then a fix is taken and the fire position triangulated with other fire spotters. Once the site is determined, a fire boss takes over and coordinates the fire fighting.

To be a fire tower lookout you must be at least 18. Lookouts usually work from dawn to dusk during the peak fire period seasons. In most areas the season lasts from mid-June until September, but in Southern California it can stretch until mid-December. Usually a lookout will be expected to work weekdays, with a relief person coming on weekends. Married couples, however, sometimes take the position for the entire fire season without relief. In truly remote areas, lookouts live at the site and have logging crews or other forest workers bring in their provisions. For their efforts, lookouts earn $14,800 per year.

There are 250 towers in all, scattered in different national forests around the country. The Forest Service has mandated that a person can only apply to one national forest per season with the application period extending from December 1 to January 15. The preferred strategy is to request the "Field Offices of the Forest Service" bulletin FS-13 from the:

U.S. Department of Agriculture
Forest Service
12th and Independence Avenues SW
P.O. Box 2417
Washington, DC 20013

After reviewing the bulletin, contact the regional offices and ask if any tower slots will be available. Select the best opening for you, write to the specific forest office, request an application, and submit it.

You may have to go through several seasons before you are assigned a tower as there is much competition for these posts. There is an interesting self-selection process at work for fire tower lookouts. If you're patient enough to wait for a job to open up, you will also be patient enough to make a good lookout once you get the job.

28 Food Stylist

Food stylists have been known to wince when somebody complains about "sour grapes." Their job, after all, is to make sure that each morsel in a food-related ad looks as perfect as if it had come from the Garden of Eden itself. Food styling has developed into a separate profession in the vast advertising industry. Stylists are responsible for making portraits of food that leap from the magazine to the stomach. For instance, they will go through trays of strawberries until they find the ONE that has just the right qualities of redness and ripeness to convey the idea of lusciousness to the American consumer. And that hamburger you see on the billboard? The crinkle in the lettuce isn't any accident. A food stylist was again at work.

As might be expected, a food stylist must have strong visual sense. A background in home economics or photography also helps. Stylists may, for instance, have to cook the turkeys that are used in ads. On-the-job training takes care of many of the technical details. Stylists usually enter the profession by assisting other food stylists or by working at one of the professional kitchens used for advertising work. Addresses and contacts for these outlets can be found via the *Creative Blackbook*, a yearly reference of who is doing what in the advertising industry. Stylists can earn over $350 per day in such cities as New York, Chicago, or Los Angeles where a lot of magazine work is done. Stylists with special expertise in such areas as dairy products may find themselves in demand nationally. As the trend towards gourmet cuisine continues, food stylists will always find a tasteful way to earn a living.

29 Foreign Service Officer

There are several ways to become an ambassador to a foreign country. Donating megabucks to a political campaign is one method. Being a golfing buddy of the President is another. A third route is to work for the foreign service division of the U.S. State Department.

Foreign service officers staff American embassies and consulates and many ambassadors are chosen from their ranks. There are many posts that need to be filled in an embassy. Political, commercial, and agricultural advisors are needed, as are public affairs personnel, security staff, secretarial staff, and visa officials. Foreign service officers are chosen from a pool of applicants who pass the annual foreign service exam. The test is administered at various federal centers around the country on the first Saturday in December. Application to take the exam must be made the preceding August or September by writing to the:

Board of Examiners
Department of State
Washington, DC 20520

If you successfully pass the written test, you would go on to take an oral exam. This exam is designed to determine how well you would function in real-life situations. Upon passing both written and oral exams, you would then be placed on a waiting list and when openings occur, you would go into a six-month training program. The program teaches basic security procedures, embassy protocols, and staff duties.

New foreign service officers start at $19,000 per year, and serve two to four years at an embassy before being rotated. Stints overseas are mixed with stateside duty.

Those seeking to become foreign service officers should be mature individuals with a broad-based education, and an aptitude for a foreign language. You should understand that working in an American embassy is often tempered by medical, food, and housing problems. But if you like to travel and enjoy experiencing different cultures, the foreign service could provide a legion of opportunities.

30 Game Show Contestant

Television game shows are the living proof of Andy Warhol's dictum that in our society everyone will be famous for 15 minutes. The game show business thrives because it fuels the American dream of acquiring instant riches without getting your hands dirty. Well, so be it. For those folks who seek their fortune at this Everyman's show business career, the best thing to do is to plan a vacation or business trip to Los Angeles and call shows listed to book a time for an interview. Don't, however, make an interview be the sole purpose of your trip. You should also plan to have a good time at the wondrous tourist traps Southern California has to offer.

The shows, their phone numbers, and the requirements are as follows:

Jeopardy – This all-time favorite show for trivia addicts can be reached by calling 213-466-3931 for an appointment. The appointments are made only two weeks in advance. Prospective contestants first take a 50-question general knowledge exam on which they must score at least 75 percent. After passing the test, applicants then play a mock version of the game and are evaluated on enthusiasm and personality. Those who are successful are placed in a contact file and may

61

be called to appear on the show anywhere from one to six months after their initial interview.

Sale of the Century – This show is produced by Reg Grundy Productions, 213-284-8644. Prospective contestants should call several weeks in advance for an interview time. Those who are successful at an initial screening interview are asked to return several days later to play a mock version of the game. The actual selection of contestants is made during this dry run. Evaluators look for people who have an outgoing personality, enthusiasm, and an ability to play the game.

Scrabble – Again, this is a Reg Grundy Productions show which can be contacted at 213-284-8644. In addition to having the aforementioned qualities of personality, you must successfully pass a Scrabble word clue test and undergo a two-hour interview process.

Password – There are some people who contend that Noah Webster played Samuel Johnson on the premier show, which attests to the phenomenal popularity "Password" has enjoyed through the aeons of television history. Produced by Mark Goodson Productions, 213-467-5100, "Password" screens its contestants based on a good vocabulary as well as presentability. Initially, 30 people play the game in a dry run, and from this group, contest evaluators can either use all of the contestants or none of them for an eventual appearance on the show.

Wheel of Fortune – Vanna White fans can contact Merv Griffin Productions at the contestant phone number 213-461-4701 for an appointment. Prospective contestants first take a five-minute written test based on the show's word puzzles. Those who pass participate in a two-hour mock version of the show while evaluators look for intelligence and a vivacious personality.

The $25,000 Pyramid – Contact Bob Stewart Productions at 213-461-3746 several weeks prior to a visit. Those who are trying out play the game against up to 30 other contestants from which several are picked for a second mock run several weeks later. Those who show a good ability to play the game and have the requisite energy and enthusiasm are placed in a contestant pool which is active for up to one year.

One other thing should be mentioned. After walking away with zillions of prize dollars, remember that the winnings are considered taxable income and the IRS will be interested in knowing about them.

31 Go-Go Dancer

"It's really glamorous in a weird sort of way," was how a go-go dancer named Louise described her profession. For prancing about a stage in a scanty costume, women and men can earn an income that ranges between $15 and $200 per night in tips plus an hourly salary of $12 to $15 per hour.

You don't necessarily have to be built like a brick lavatory to succeed in this field. "Most of the girls who are successful smile a lot on stage and make eye contact with the customers," Louise said. "Although some girls are professional dancers, you don't have to have any kind of ballet training. Some make their own costumes or bring in their own music for routines. In a way, you can get really creative as a dancer." The creativity also extends to choosing a stage name, but Louise suggested that you choose a name carefully, since you're likely to get stuck with it permanently.

A dancer usually works 30 minutes on stage and is off for 30 minutes. Some bars require that dancers use their free time to hustle drinks from customers. "The main function of the dancer is to keep the customer drinking," Louise said.

The constant exposure to drinking and cigarette smoke takes its toll. In addition, the generally sleazy atmosphere of go-go bars tends to create a depressing funk.

"The teasing quality of the dancer generates for some

guys a reality that will never happen. It could be dangerous if you aren't careful," Louise said.

Male dancers don't have the physical danger to worry about and there is a different atmosphere to the places in which they perform. Most male dancers are personable hunks who generate roaring enthusiasm from their female crowds. Cliff, who has been a dancer for four years, said, "For most women it's a good time, but I always wonder about some."

It pays for a dancer to enter the field with a bit of savvy. Dancers can find a first job by scanning newspaper ads. Afterwards, you learn by word of mouth which joints are classier.

A dancer should know why he or she is up on stage. If it's to earn cash in a hurry, so be it. But the ease with which money can be made is in itself a trap. You should also be thinking of a future life. As Louise noted, "There is nothing sadder than a go-go dancer past her prime."

32 Graphologist

The moving hand having writ moves on . . . and leaves behind a very revealing insight into your character and personality. Graphology involves using a sample of a person's handwriting as a type of "body language" to detect character traits. In that context, many corporations are hiring graphologists to assist them in making hiring decisions. Graphologists are paid between $100 and $400 for this type of consultation. One advantage that the method offers, according to the International Graphoanalysis Society, is that it can provide character analysis without relying on tests that may be discriminatory.

Prospective graphologists usually start by contacting the:

International Graphoanalysis Society
111 North Canal Street
Chicago, IL 60606

The Society offers an 18-month home study course. Loops, swirls, slants, and other refinements of handwriting are focused upon and correlated with corresponding character traits.

An eye for detail is necessary along with a good business sense. Sheila Kurtz, owner of A New Slant in New York City, explained that graphoanalysts are in a service profession and must build their business accordingly. They should have the public relations skills that are necessary to convince corporate executives, social

workers, psychologists, and others in the human services professions of the graphologist's valuable slant on
life.

33 Gunsmith

A gunsmith is a craftsman whose work must be right on target. Working with components such as sights, swivels, and gun barrels, a gunsmith customizes a weapon to the specifications of its future owner.

Gunsmiths learn their craft at technical schools located around the country. Many schools can be located through ads appearing in the magazine *American Rifleman.* Instructor Dave Defenbaugh said students at his school, Pine Technical Institute in Pine City, Minnesota, receive nearly 2,100 hours of training in two nine-month-long semesters. "During school they learn how to modify sights, fit the barrel, carve the stock, and the dozen other procedures that are involved in fabricating a rifle or shotgun," Defenbaugh noted. Emphasis is also placed on licensing regulations and repair work.

Depending on the intricacies of the engraving, a customized firearm takes a minimum of 100 hours to make. The price for such a weapon ranges from $2,500 to $10,000, and dedicated trap shooters, target shooters, hunters and collectors create a demand for those pieces, according to gunsmith George Beitzinger of New York City.

Defenbaugh said gunsmiths are mostly an independent lot who go into business for themselves after they receive their training. As for salary, Defenbaugh estimated that if you work in a shop, a typical beginning salary is betweem $5 and $10 per hour. After you've established a reputation as a gunsmith, you can name your own figure for a handmade firearm. Reputation is very important, since a poorly fitted chamber can literally blow a rifleman's head off. Liability insurance is a distinct downside of the profession, as is the need for costly machinery such as metal lathes and drill presses.

Offsetting these factors is the personal satisfaction that comes from being creative with your hands as well as your head. "Gunsmithing is a labor of love," Defenbaugh said. "Most of my students tell me they are finally doing what they want to do. To be good, a person should be mechanically oriented, patient, and coordinated."

Skill, training, dedication–if a gunsmith possesses these, he is certain to have a good shot at success in this field.

34 Herbalist

Healing with herbs is one of mankind's earliest approaches to medicine. Herbalists are men and women who study and utilize plants for their curative powers. There are people from all walks of life who see herbal medicine as a vital adjunct to modern clinical practice, and when they need advice, they seek out an herbalist.

There are several paths you can take to become an herbalist. The first is to formally study the subject matter. One of the few schools teaching herbal medicine is the:

School for Herbal Medicine
148 Forest Avenue
Tumbridge Wells, Kent, England

Students who attend learn plant identification and use, along with human physiology and botany. There is a school in America that teaches the use of herbs. It is the:

California School of Herbal Studies
P.O. Box 39
Forestville, CA 95436

There are also workshops held at various progressive teaching centers around the country.

You can also apprentice yourself to an established herbalist and/or study on your own. Herbalists can often be located through New Age bookstores and centers. A particularly good book with which to start your

70

own reading program is *The Herb Book* by John Lust. It is available in paperback and is extensively cross-indexed.

Once you have a working knowledge of herbs, there are different ways to practice the art. One method is to become a wildcrafter–a person who collects and processes herbs for medical use and commercial resale. Plants are not the only item wildcrafters gather. In the Rocky Mountain region there is a market for elk horns, which are shed each season by male elk. The horns are ground into powder and sold to exporters who send the horn powder to the Far East, where the substance is valued as an aphrodisiac.

Herbalists also maintain shops and mail-order businesses which sell wide varieties of herbs and teas. Many herbalists also practice acupuncture or operate in conjunction with acupuncturists.

A third aspect of herbal practice is to become a consultant. New York herbalist Edward Berk explained that a consultant assist clients in the choice of herbal preparations that will most benefit their physical conditions. They also present seminars and lectures to further educate the public in the use of herbs in healing.

How substantial an income you can earn as an herbalist will depend to a large extent on your initiative. Suffice to say that there are herbalists employed throughout the country. Americans are becoming increasingly aware of alternative methods of health care, and are thus rediscovering the wisdom of the folk rhyme, "For every ache and pain of man, there's a plant to cure it in God's master plan."

71

35 Holographer

The mystery, beauty, and wonder of holography is just beginning to be appreciated in this country. It is a magical art form that is coming to life through the vision of men and women who are tripping the light fantastic.

Holographer Dan Schweitzer of New York City said the medium uses laser beams to record three-dimensional objects on a sensitized glass plate. When the plate is developed it then recreates the three-dimensional image. Since there are five Nobel Prize-winning concepts that are part of holography's technical side, any further explanation of the process is best summarized by simply saying it is magic.

It is magic that can be learned. Schweitzer said an artistic background is helpful although you do not need any prior scientific or photographic experience to begin a career as an holographer. A listing of schools and individuals that teach courses in the field can be obtained from the:

Holography Directory
Museum of Holography
11 Mercer Street
New York, NY 10013

The New York Holographic Laboratories, for instance, conducts an intensive two-weekend course that provides people with the fundamentals to develop their own styles. The basic theory behind holography is explained and students spend the rest of their class time making and developing holographs.

Following these sessions, an artist can then consider establishing a studio. Schweitzer noted that a person can obtain the necessary equipment to create professional-quality holographs for about $1,000. Sources of supply can be found in the reference book *Laser Focus Buying Guide.*

As for earning a living, holographers create displays for trade shows, work closely with advertising agencies, and sell their works of art through galleries and museums. Salary is dependent upon ability and reputation.

Holography is the next giant step that art will take. Its potential has hardly been touched. It beckons people of ordinary physique who are distinguished by extraordinary dreams.

36 Hospice Worker

Whether we choose to go quietly into the night, or to rage against the dying of the light, death is the one experience all of us will someday share. Since 1974, there has been a movement known as the hospice philosophy that seeks to provide support and care for people in the final phases of a terminal disease so that they can live out the balance of their lives, however short that might be, as fully and as comfortably as possible. Currently there are over 4,000 hospices in the United States. The majority focus their efforts on helping patients who are dying of cancer, but a growing number are now assisting patients who are dying of AIDS. A complete listing of hospices can be obtained from the:

National Hospice Organization
Suite 307
1901 North Fort Myer Drive
Arlington, VA 22209

An interdisciplinary team of nurses, doctors, clergymen, social workers, and volunteers staff the hospices. Their mission is to formulate a treatment plan for both the patient and his or her family. Of these professionals, the nurses and social workers are the only ones involved on a full-time basis, and their salary is commensurate with experience. Doctors and clergymen assist the hospices as part of their other responsibilities.

"Often the pain comes from many directions–physical, spiritual, and emotional. This is why we must cross many barriers," said Maureen Bryden of the Phelps Memorial Hospice. Ms. Bryden said that when she selects members for her hospice team, one of the key factors she looks for is a good sense of humor. "It's the best antidote against burnout," she said. It helps, too, if the person has a positive attitude and a rounded, balanced life, since the experience of confronting death on a regular basis demands a great deal of inner strength. Hospice workers must also be flexible, since the nature of their work dictates that set appointments cannot always be kept.

Being a hospice worker is demanding, but at the same time, it can bring great personal satisfaction. Ms. Bryden said that most people involved with the program are very idealistic and highly dedicated. "It's the final opportunity," she said, "to affirm the individuality of every human being."

37 Hypnotist

The idea of hypnotism is a mesmerizing one. By getting a person to quiet their conscious mind, it opens a door to the subconscious that may otherwise be barricaded by the hustle and bustle of daily life.

Hypnotism is a skill that can be easily learned, but to become proficient requires much dedication. In the hands of a competent hypnotist, it is a valuable tool that can be used to help people allay fears, overcome phobias, and change counter-productive behavior. It is commonly used to help people stop smoking, lose weight, and improve memory.

About 97 percent of the population can be hypnotized and the basic skills can be learned in as little as 14 hours, according to Dr. Daniel Lutzker of the Milton H. Erikson Institute of Hypnosis in New York City. "Each hypnotist evolves his or her own style, but you certainly do not need a shiny pendulum to hypnotize people," he said.

Many medium and large-size cities have Yellow Page listings for hypnotists. Seminars are held throughout the country where you can learn the skills. In addition, a book entitled *Hypnosis Questions and Answers*, edited by Martin Segall, explains many aspects of the practice.

Although almost anyone can learn to be a hypnotist, the question arises as to what you do with the knowledge afterwards. Dr. Lutzker suggests that it is best used as an ancillary skill for health care and social work professionals. "It's more of a technique than a profession. It allows a practitioner to get to a deep level with a patient," he said.

Hypnotists earn $50 and upwards per hour, depending on whether or not they are combining it with other forms of treatment. According to Stanley Mitchell, executive director of the International Guild of Hypnotists, hypnotism is an unregulated and unlicensed practice in this country. Mitchell suggested that if you are just interested in the practice of hypnotism, it is possible to work with referrals from medical practitioners. This also allows you to develop a clientele of your own. "About 70 percent of my practice comes from word-of-mouth referrals, 25 percent from medical practitioners, and 5 percent from the street," he said. For more information on the field, he suggested contacting one of the following:

International Guild of Hypnotists
410 South Michigan Avenue
Chicago, IL 60605

Association to Advance Ethical Hypnosis
2500 East Hallandale Beach Boulevard
Hallandale, FL 33009

Both organizations have conventions and meetings throughout the country where members exchange information and techniques.

A few hypnotists go into show business and perform onstage. To do this, you must be a superb showman, since you must rely on members of the audience to participate. Inducing a hypnotic trance will certainly not be sufficient. "There is no stock show in a hypnotism stage act," explained performer Leonard Gladstone of New York. "The props are the people."

38 Indexer

A librarian once said, "A book without an index is like a body without a soul." A bit strong perhaps, but when it comes to books, librarians usually do have strong opinions. On the other hand, the librarian may be right, since an index makes it possible to quickly locate information in a book. Imagine trying to look up all references to Benjamin Franklin in a textbook on American History without the aid of an index! The person who creates this time-saving device is an indexer.

Most indexers work at home as freelancers. Some may work through companies specializing in editorial work (see Editorial Services in the Yellow Pages). After the indexer has made a contract with a publisher, the publisher will send galley proofs or rough page proofs of the book to be indexed. The indexer then carefully and thoroughly reads each page, marking pertinent words and phrases, and noting themes as they appear. These notes are then either entered into a computer (the modern method) or jotted onto index cards (the time-honored method) and then alphabetized and organized at the end of the project.

Indexer Jean Agee of Silver Spring, Maryland, said it takes from two to four weeks to index a 300-page book, for which an indexer receives a flat rate per page, a flat rate per job, or an hourly rate of $15 to $20 per hour.

There are several ways to establish oneself as an indexer. The first is to become recognized as an authority in one's field. For instance, a chemist would be familiar with the terms and technical data that of necessity would appear in a chemistry text. People with expertise in any special field or who have a strong background in English can send an "I'm available" letter to the publishers listed in references such as *Literary Market Place* or *The International Directory of Little Magazines and Small Presses*. Running an ad in trade publications such as *Publisher's Weekly* is also helpful.

Another option is to join the:

American Society of Indexers
1700 18th Street NW
Washington, DC 20009

Members of the society are listed in an annual "Register of Indexers," and Society president Ben-Ami Lipetz suggested that those interested in the profession should attend the society's annual meetings to get a first-hand familiarity with the process. Although the society does not at present sponsor seminars, there are courses on indexing available at schools offering degrees in library sciences.

There will be an increasing demand for indexers in the future as the information explosion keeps exploding. Ms. Agee said not only are there opportunities to index books, but indexers are now being hired to index periodicals, conference proceedings, and professional catalogs.

A person most suited to this field is one who has an eye for detail and who enjoys reading. A prime advantage is that you can work at home, since publishers ship the galley proofs anywhere in the country. But as with almost all freelancers, you're at the mercy of a feast or famine work schedule. Another disadvantage is the tightness of deadline pressure. An indexer is the last person in the editorial chain, and if there are any delays earlier along the line, they can cut into the time available to complete a project, leaving the indexer on the short end. Offsetting this is the variety of work involved, because an indexer will encounter everything from A to Z.

39 Interpreter for the Deaf

The sound of silence is a daily reality for thousands of deaf people. But thanks to a growing number of interpreters for the deaf, their lives do not have to be ones of quiet desperation.

Interpreters for the deaf are helping to open many economic and educational doors that were closed to deaf people in the past. For instance, there is an effort being made to mainstream deaf children into regular classes, instead of bundling them off to a state school for the deaf. This means that an interpreter accompanies the child to all of his/her classes and acts as a conduit for communication between the student and the teacher and the rest of the class. There are also corporate programs to train deaf workers. The interpreter again relays information back and forth between the deaf person and the training officer.

To enter this field, a person should have a strong desire to work with people, since it is almost exclusively a people-oriented profession. In addition, a person should have a facility for languages, good hand-eye coordination, and fine motor skill ability, since there is a need to rapidly transfer speech into motion, according to Don Renzulli, who coordinates the deaf interpreter evaluation program.

The training for an interpreter begins at one of the universities or community colleges across the country that teach deaf interpretation. A list of courses is available from:

Interpreters for the Deaf, Inc.
1 Metro Square
51 Monroe Street, Suite 1107
Rockville, MD 20850

Interpreters must master sign language, pidgin signed English, and the manual alphabet, and must understand the ethics of interpretation. After their training, they must pass a proficiency exam before being added to the National Registry of Interpreters for the Deaf.

Interpreters earn about $8.50 per hour plus benefits if they work regularly for schools, or up to $35 per hour doing freelance work. Interpreting can be fatiguing but also challenging, since the information and the clients keep changing. As our society opens more doors to its handicapped citizens, interpreters for the deaf will be needed to extend helping hands.

40 Jewelry Worker

Set this book down for a second and look at the next person who walks past. The chances are that he or she is wearing a piece of jewelry. Earrings, bracelets, and necklaces have been with us ever since some cave dweller decided their outfit really needed a mastodon-bone pendant. Indeed, jewelry is a zillion-dollar-a-year business and has enough flexibility so that it can provide a golden opportunity to individuals with a variety of skills and abilities.

For those who like to work with their hands, there is the opportunity to train as a silversmith or a goldsmith. This profession involves fashioning either jewelry or practical objects, such as plates or bowls, out of precious metals. New York City gemologist and smith Paul J. Weisbroat recommended that you contact the fine arts department of a university in your region and learn the requisite skills through a bachelor of fine arts program. If you cannot find such a program in your area, one is offered at the:

Fashion Institute of Technology
227 West 27th Street
New York, NY 10001

Smiths learn basic techniques such as hammering and annealing along with artistic design. Weisbroat estimated that you can learn the basic skills within six months at a concentrated program. Afterwards it could take a lifetime to refine and fully develop your talents.

According to Weisbroat, smiths need patience, manual dexterity, and the ability to perceive spatial dimensions.

After mastering the basics, smiths have the option of apprenticing under more experienced smiths or going into business for themselves. The latter requires an investment of several thousand dollars for the necessary metals, tools, and furnaces. As for income levels, it is dependent on your artistry, talent, and reputation.

Closely related to the talent of working with metals is that of inlaying precious stones in metal to create jewelry. Working with precious stones, and grading and appraising them, is the focus of the Gemological Institute of America (GIA) which has a branch in New York City and a main campus at the:

Gemological Institute of America
1660 Stewart Street
Santa Monica, CA 90404

The GIA program is internationally known and teaches students how to recognize, grade, and appraise diamonds and precious stones in its six-month program. Students need not have any prior exposure to the gem business to apply, but they should have good eyesight and strong academic skills, since the studies are quite rigorous. With a GIA degree, a person is qualified to serve as an insurance appraiser. Other career options include sales, design, grading, and importing.

If you want to market your own creations or the jewelry made by others, you can sell jewelry through various outlets—craft fairs, home shows, flea markets, stores, mail order. etc. There is at least a 100 percent markup on jewelry, so a modest investment in raw materials or wholesale jewelry can go a long way. Individuals who choose this route usually deal with several manufacturers and importers. Your own personality and taste usually determine the lines of jewelry you will want to handle. You can find hundreds of wholesalers under one roof at the various jewelry trade shows held throughout the country. Each major market area usually has at least one show per year. The times and dates can be obtained from any major city's convention bureau. The largest shows of all are held in New York City at the Jacob Javits Convention Center. For exact dates contact the:

New York Convention and Visitors Bureau
2 Columbus Circle
New York, NY 10019

To attend these shows all you need is a business card that shows you are affiliated with some phase of the retailing business. Such a card can afford you an entry to a profitable and stylish future.

41 **Kibbutznik**

The Israeli kibbutz movement has been described as a community motivated by ideals rather than an ideal community. High ideals they are. The residents of the 250 kibbutzim that exist in Israel share in the belief in equality, the dignity of work, and in the spirit of democracy.

Some kibbutzim focus on industry, others on agriculture, but in either case they welcome the opportunity to share their unique way of life with volunteers from around the world. Indeed, the sharing goes both ways. As Joel Magid wrote in the book, *Kibbutz:The Way We Live*, "Through them, [the volunteers] our children and young members see a world they wouldn't otherwise know, with all its temptations, conceptions and opportunities."

The opportunity to work on a kibbutz is open to all individuals, regardless of religious affiliation or knowledge of Hebrew as a language. Most people participate in the temporary program which is aimed at volunteers aged 18 to 32 who agree to a four- to six-week kibbutz stay. A second structure is the *ulpan* program. It is aimed at older professionals who can stay four to six months on a kibbutz and who sometimes stay on permanently. The *ulpan* program is also intended to provide those of Jewish faith the chance to affirm their heritage and explore more deeply the Jewish faith.

Both programs are coordinated by the:

Kibbutz Aliya Desk
27 West 20th Street
New York, NY 10011

This office is the first stop for kibbutz volunteers. Here applicants are interviewed and the necessary medical and personnel forms are processed. Once you are approved by the New York office, you travel at your own expense to Tel Aviv, where the Israeli branch of the kibbutz movement assigns you to a site where volunteers are needed.

Once at a kibbutz, you join in the economic life of the community and are assigned a task such as picking fruit, washing laundry, preparing food, etc. No prior skills are necessary, since old members will teach the new volunteers the tasks at hand. Workdays usually last six to eight hours, and the workweek is usually six days. Although you receive no salary, physical needs, such as food, housing, and laundry, are all taken care of while you are at the kibbutz. You will also share in the celebrations and cultural activities of the community.

An ideal way of life? Well, it could be. Since there is a constant influx of volunteers, however, it is difficult for permanent members and newcomers to feel real attachment for each other. Security is another consideration. Many kibbutzim are located on Israel's frontiers, so it is advisable to plan your stay during periods of relative calm in the Mideast. But if you want to experience life in a different culture, then the Israeli kibbutzim are ready to say *shalom!*

42 Lampworker

This is an old-fashioned name for a very up-to-date profession. Lampworkers are the men and women who fabricate custom glassware for scientific laboratories.

The primary school that teaches this craft is the:

Salem Community College
Carneys Point, NJ 08069-2799

Students who attend the two-year course learn such subjects as blueprint reading and design, techniques of glassblowing, repair of laboratory glass, and glass lathe operation.

Manual dexterity is necessary for a person to become proficient in this craft, since molten glass can be a tricky substance to work with. Other than that, the rules of good common sense apply, since open flames and jagged edges are part and parcel of the trade. Lampworkers are attached to the field because they like to work with both their hands and their brains. The Salem program has an extensive placement service, and its graduates work in both industrial and university labs. Salaries for lampworkers range between $5 and $20 per hour, depending on experience.

Glassbending is an allied field. Glassbenders create the neon signs that are used for advertising and artistic purposes. Glassbenders work with four-foot long sections of glass tubing that range in thickness from 8 to 25 millimeters. The glass tubing is heated to soften it, while the bender is all the while blowing a stream of air through the section to keep it from collapsing. Once it is pliable, the tubing is shaped to the intended design by laying it on a sketch of the design placed on a table. When all the sections are shaped and the lengths are fused together, an inert gas such as neon or argon is injected into the tubing via a vacuum pump, and the tube is electrically charged so that the desired glowing effect is achieved.

Hugh Elliott, owner of Neon Design Associates in New York City, said that it takes experience and practice before you develop a sense of how the glass is heating and when it should be bent. If you are interested in becoming a glassblower, Elliott recommended that you visit a sign shop first to see the process firsthand. Then you learn the basics by taking classes or by apprenticing yourself to a skilled glassbender. One of the foremost schools teaching glassbending is

Northern Advertising, Inc.
P.O. Box 92
Antigo, WI 54409

After you learn the basics, the next step is to contact individual firms to get an entry-level position as a sign installer, and then to practice glassbending during free time or after work under the tutelage of an experienced bender. Salary as a glassbender depends upon skill, and experienced craftspeople earn around $20 per hour.

Elliott said drafting ability and manual dexterity are helpful in this profession. One great advantage to glassbending is that it will never be taken over by some programmed robot, since each tube must be individually shaped. With a 40-color range now possible, neon will increasingly become the sign of the times.

43 Massage Therapist

During the past decade, Americans have become increasingly aware that good health involves more than just taking a few pills. This realization that the body must be treated as a whole organism has given rise to a number of holistic health professions, massage therapy being one of them.

Both men and women can be massage therapists. Many enter the profession after having discovered the invigorating benefits of a massage themselves. Massage is a way of relaxing muscles and releasing tension. As a result, it provides a sense of both physical and mental well-being.

There are schools and institutes throughout the nation that teach massage. A listing of facilities can be obtained from the:

American Massage Therapy Institute
P.O. Box 1270
Kingsport, TN 37662

The courses cover a great deal about body mechanics and structure. At the Chicago School for Massage Therapy, for instance, students learn anatomy, sports massage, deep tissue massage, and related subjects during a three-semester program. There are also specific disciplines within the field of massage. Two that are currently popular are shiatsu and rolfing.

The Japanese technique of shiatsu resembles acupuncture but without the needles. Instead, pressure is applied by a practitioner's hands to rebalance a client's energy field. A leading school for the technique is the:

Ohashi Institute
12 West 27th Street
New York, NY 10001

Rolfing is a technique for realigning the body. It is taught at

The Rolf Institute
302 Pearl Street
Boulder, Colorado 80306

In addition to providing general toning massages, therapists are usually trained to provide for very specific problems, such as lower back pain or wrenched shoulders. For this reason, most states require you to pass a licensing exam before you can begin a practice. The market for massage therapists is currently expanding. Many set up a private practice. Others are employed by health clubs, training spas, or chiropractic clinics. A massage averages $35 and lasts about one hour. Because of the amount of concentration required by the practitioner, 25 to 30 massages is usually the maximum number that can be given in a week.

Those who are successful in this field have a deep respect for individuals in particular and the human body in general. For massage therapists, reaching out to touch someone means exactly that.

44 Midwife

Midwifery dates back to the dawn of mankind, and today is enjoying a life-giving renewal in this country as women are becoming more conscious of their emotional as well as medical needs during pregnancy.

The essential role of the midwife is that of a physical and emotional advisor to pregnant women. Within this position lies a broad range of variables concerning the training, licensing, and moral role of the midwife.

Although there are some male midwifes, this is primarily a woman's field. Certified nurse-midwife Maria Corsaro of New York City especially enjoys the broad range of possibilities it offers. "Midwifery incorporates elements of the scientific, spiritual, philosophical, artistic, and political spheres," she said. There are several paths that a woman can follow to become a practicing midwife.

The most widely recognized route is that of obtaining a professional nursing education. This involves attending nursing school and studying such courses as anatomy, biology, and psychology, and gaining clinical experience in such areas as surgery, community health, and pediatrics. This training culminates in a Registered Nurse (RN) degree, after which a year of further study in the birthing process would lead to a master's degree with a midwife emphasis. Approved schools are listed with the:

American College of Nurse Midwifes
1522 K Street NW, Suite 1120
Washington, DC 20005

Following her schooling, she would then take a professional certification exam offered by this body. The certification is important, since it is recognized or required by 45 states. Upon being certified, a midwife then has the option of becoming a member of a hospital staff, working for a physician, working at a birthing center, or specializing in home births. In general, annual salaries for nurse-midwifes are in the $20,000 plus range.

But what about the other states?

Since the process of birth is certainly not a diseased state, it falls through a loophole under several jurisdictions in the American medical-legal system that regulates the practice of medicine. Many states–Texas, New Mexico, Mississippi, and Tennessee, for instance–allow the practice of lay midwifery that does not include a formal nursing degree. A full list of states with these provisions is available from the American College of Nurse Midwifes. In these states a woman would train under a midwife or doctor, and although she would not be allowed to prescribe drugs or engage in surgical procedures, she would assist births in the way "granny women" have for centuries. One hitch in this method is that insurance companies do not reimburse lay midwifes. So lay midwifes must rely on a barter system or on direct payment for their services. As for successful birth rates, certified nurse-midwife Virginia Jackson said that lay midwifes compare favorably with physicians. "The important things for a trouble-free birth are the prenatal care and the skill of the attendant," she noted.

The resurgence of midwifes comes at a favorable time, since births are on the increase and the number of doctors involved with obstetrics is decreasing due to the high cost malpractice insurance and malpractice suits. An interesting statistic that Ms. Corsaro observed was that 60 percent of doctors are sued for malpractice whereas only 6 percent of midwifes are sued. Due to their emphasis on the birth process, midwifes will be on the cutting edge of such innovative techniques as underwater birthing. They will be an integral part of medicine's future, as they have been of its past.

45 Miniature Golf Pro

There is an old adage on the professional golf tour–"You drive for show and putt for dough." Well, as a professional miniature golfer, forget the drive part–the whole game is centered around the skill of putting.

Professional miniature golf was born in 1960, and is in a large part the creation of Putt-Putt Golf Courses of America™, upon whose courses the tournaments are held. The 54-hole tournaments are held on weekends throughout the country, with Ohio, New York, the Carolinas, Oklahoma, Florida, Texas, and Virginia being hotbeds of activity. The tournaments came under the aegis of the:

Professional Putters Association
P.O. Box 35237
3007 Ft. Bragg Road
Fayetteville, NC 28303

Winners of local and regional tournaments, some of which are televised, can collect several thousand dollars in prizes, while the winner of the national tournament can pocket up to $16,000 in prize money. This adds up to a nice second income that can be had for the fun of it.

Most professional putters develop their proficiency by playing in amateur tournaments. To become a pro, you need a letter of recommendation from a course manager, after which you become a member of the circuit. Tournaments average about 50 participants, and the course can usually be completed within two hours.

But the shortness of time belies the tension that is involved. Champion putter Mark Coup of Columbus, Ohio, said the pressure of competition is always present. "A few bad putts and it's all over," he said. Coup added that in addition to (hopefully) winning some prize money, you will also form friendships across the country. The prize purses are not large, but neither are the expenses. After all, with only one club, a putter does not need to worry about hiring a caddy.

46 Miss America

"Here she comes, Miss America . . ." The opening of that song is as familiar as "The Star Spangled Banner." Perhaps even more so, since there is always a beautiful and talented young lady associated with it.

Miss America, no matter what ups and downs the pageant has had, is very much an American cultural icon. She is selected each fall in Atlantic City, and thousands of television viewers across the country hope that the beauty from their state will be chosen fairest of the fair, or at least Miss Congeniality.

The basic requirements are quite straightforward. An entrant must be a female, between the ages of 17 and 26, a high school graduate, single and never married, of good moral character, and a citizen of the United States. Joan Jones, executive director of the New York pageant, said there is no single route to follow to become Miss America. Some girls reach the goal after entering numerous local beauty pageants to bolster their self-confidence and gain experience. Other Miss Americas are just born.

The first step in the Miss America process is to contact

Karen E. Aarons, Executive Secretary
Miss America Pageant
Atlantic City, NJ 08401

The central office will give you the name and address of the pageant coordinator in your own state. The next step is to participate in the state-level pageants, which may include several regional pageants to narrow the field. Young ladies are judged on the following basis: 50 percent for talent, 25 percent for swimsuit appearance, 12.5 percent for evening gown appearance, and 12.5 percent for the personal interview. Although there is no entry fee charged a participant, she must have her own gown and swimsuit. In reality, expenses do mount up. Besides buying clothing, most contestants spend a good deal of money on coaches, lessons, hairdressers, and whatever else it takes to build the right image.

Winners of the state pageants are sent to Atlantic City for final judging, with all expenses paid. There, after days of nervousness, giggling, and hoopla, the new Miss America is crowned for her one-year reign as America's queen.

There is a fair chunk of change involved in the beauty queen business. Miss America herself receives $30,000 with runners-up and semi-finalists also receiving at least $4,000 apiece in scholarships or cash. Even on the state level, winners receive varying amounts of scholarships, anywhere from $2,000 to $15,000. The winning is nice, but as Ms. Jones pointed out, "Then the work begins!" Miss America is booked an average of 340 days a year and, Ms. Jones said, she must always look her best. "She has to forget about blue jeans for a year." State winners also serve at functions throughout their home state, earning between $200 and $350 per appearance.

The qualities that a girl needs to become Miss America go beyond beauty and talent. Since her primary purpose is to serve in a public relations position, she must be personable and intelligent. A lot of ambition also helps. Girls enter the pageant for a variety of reasons. Some do it for the scholarship funds, others for the ego gratification. Still others enter because way back in their childhood they pictured themselves walking down the runway to the crooning of "Here she comes, Miss America."

47 Monk/Nun

The profession of being a contemplative monk or nun, more properly termed a calling, involves a high degree of personal commitment. The move towards this vocation usually occurs when your worldly cup is full and deep spiritual longings need to be realized. At this time, you may be irresistibly drawn to the life of a monk or nun.

There are communities throughout the country that are open to those who seek to deliberately distance themselves from the world at large. Both the Catholic and Buddhist religions have a strong tradition of contemplative communities. The quiet and peace of these monasteries provide the setting that is necessary to develop the spirit within.

For Catholics, there is the Trappist order for men and the Dominican order for women. Both have centers throughout the country. Emphasis is placed both on prayer and the activities that are needed to keep the community functioning. The day usually includes a full cycle of prayers, beginning at 5 a.m. and ending in the early evening. The combination of communal prayer, solitude, and vigorous activity such as farming, baking bread, gardening, and tending bees provide a harmonious, simple lifestyle that assists in spiritual growth.

Since the monastic life is a radical departure from conventional life, a period of time is set aside during which both the community and the individual learn more about each other before a final commitment is made. For instance, the Trappists call for a 30-day trial period, followed by two years as a novitiate, three to four years of temporary vows, and finally, solemn profession for life. Incidentally, an individual does not have to be a priest to be a monk.

To learn more about the Catholic orders, one can find a listing of monasteries in a copy of the *Catholic Almanac*, which is available at almost all rectories and religious bookstores. Some centers maintain guest houses where it is possible to visit for an extended retreat and sample the life firsthand.

For Buddhists, there is a more flexible time schedule involved before you are ordained a monk or nun. A center's abbot will observe your commitment and spiritual growth through the years and determine when you have progressed enough to take your vows. For Zen monks and nuns, meditation is an important feature of their lives. Genro, a Buddhist monk, explained that meditation does not always produce the bliss that is often associated with it. It can, in fact, be quite painful as hidden emotions and memories rise to the surface and demand resolution. For this reason, the life of a monk or nun in either tradition can be quite difficult. There are no distractions such as movies or vacations that you can use to avoid facing personal revelations. There is only you and God.

There are Buddhist centers scattered throughout the country and they can be located via the Yellow Pages of a phone book.

Those who are considering a monastic life would do well to examine their motives in choosing this path. You should not be running from something. You should be running towards something.

48 Nanny

It takes a bit more to be a nanny today than the ability to say "Supercalifragilisticexpialadocious." The good old days of flying umbrellas have given way to a sense of professionalism and pride that mark the rebirth of this traditional method of caring for children.

As more women are achieving high-paying positions in the work force, more two-paycheck families are finding they can afford to consider several options in the career vs. family dilemma. Employing a nanny is emerging as one viable way to provide individual loving attention to a child while the mother is working.

The ideal nanny is not a ninny. The position is that of surrogate parent to a child or children. She (or in some cases, he) must be a sensible, stable individual who loves children. Most prospective nannies are recent college graduates with a background in early child development. Activities such as camp counseling and babysitting also help to round out a nanny's resume. Due to the increasing popularity of the profession, schools are also offering courses in such areas as parent-nanny relationships. A listing of such schools can be obtained from the:

American Council of Nanny Schools
c/o Joy Shelton
Delta College
University Center, MI 49710

Nannies can locate families through school placement services and via classified ads appearing in large city newspapers. Most contracts specify at least a one-year commitment to the job. Since many parents employ nannies when their child is young, this year can be spent changing a lot of diapers.

But there are benefits. Nannies usually average $200 per week in salary, have room and board provided, and enjoy the opportunity to travel with the family. A side benefit is the chance to make valuable personal and professional contacts through the host family.

Before running off to the nearest record store to buy a Julie Andrews album, consider that Americans do not have the knack of handling household staff that the English do. It takes willpower and assertiveness to keep from being drawn into the household life as a domestic servant. You may sign on intending to provide child care and wind up polishing silverware. Another downside is that it is very easy to get wrapped up in the life of the family to the exclusion of developing a circle of your own friends.

An interesting aspect of the profession is that older "granny nannies" are in great demand. If you have raised several children, prospective employers will likely be willing to overlook the fact that you do not have a degree in child psychology!

49 Parade Float Maker

Everyone loves a parade, especially those folks whose job it is to create the flower-bedecked floats that cruise the parade routes to the delight of all the spectators. This is one profession where college partying is actually an asset. The time spent building floats for the homecoming game can give a person skills needed to construct floats on a professional basis.

Float makers work with designers to turn fantasy into reality. It may take between 1,200 and 1,500 man-hours to build a float. Rudolph Erlich, former owner of Bond Parade Floats of New Jersey, said that people who work on parade floats are jacks-of-all-trades. They are artistically inclined and also have carpentry, painting, electrical, and plumbing skills. Most of the training is done on the job. For their efforts, float makers earn between $25,000 and $30,000 a year.

Erlich said most float companies are based near cities noted for parades, for instance, Pasadena, New Orleans, and New York City. Those interested in pursuing this career can scan local Yellow Pages to find the nearest float maker, or better yet, find one by going to a parade!

50 Peace Corps Volunteer

They call it "the toughest job you'll ever love," and in many ways it is. Both the Marshall Plan and the Peace Corps were truly altruistic programs that were implemented as part of American foreign policy. The Marshall Plan has long since expired, having served its purpose, but the Peace Corps, which was established in 1961 by President John F. Kennedy, continues its work to this day. At present there are over 6,000 volunteers serving two-year commitments in 62 countries around the world. Wherever they are assigned, the men and women of the Peace Corps are involved with helping local people create and carry out such programs as planting trees, keeping bees, teaching diesel mechanics, and promoting health care.

Although the emphasis is on skilled professionals, last year the Peace Corps enrolled nearly 500 persons (22 percent of its recruitment) as generalists with liberal arts backgrounds. Volunteers came from a cross section of American life. Some are just out of college while others have taken a mid-career sabbatical or are entering after retirement.

To join the Peace Corps, the first step is to request an information packet and application by writing the:

Peace Corps
P-301
Washington, DC 20526

Upon completion of the forms and acceptance into the

program, you undergo an eight- to twelve-week training program in the country to which you are assigned. You will study their language and culture and the skills appropriate to your job. When you have been assigned to a project, you will either live with a host family or in housing at the level of the people with whom you will be working. A monthly allowance is provided while you are "in country," and at the end of your stay, you will receive a readjustment payment of $175 for each month of service.

It is not an easy life. When you are living at subsistence levels, it really means subsistence. Volunteers can usually bet on contracting some intestinal ailment during their tour, and at times the isolation from the U.S. of A. can be overwhelming.

Why then, have more than 120,000 Americans joined the Peace Corps over its 25-year history? For some, it is a sense of adventure. For others, it is a sense of sharing. But for whatever reason, it is reassuring to note that in this decade of rampant greed, there are some individuals who still harken to President Kennedy's message: "To those peoples in huts and villages of half the globe struggling to break the bonds of mass misery, we pledge our best efforts to help them help themselves . . ."

51 Perfumer

William Shakespeare could never have made it in the perfume business, not after writing such drivel as "That which we call a rose by any other name would smell as sweet." Neither could Gertrude Stein with "A rose is a rose is a rose is a rose." What was the matter with the woman? Did she have a sinus condition?

For perfumers, a rose is much more than a pretty flower. It is the essence of allure, romance, and a host of other emotions that are triggered by our olfactory nerves. Perfuming is big business in this country. Not only are perfumes sold for cosmetic purposes, but scents are added to air fresheners, soaps, candles, and innumerable other products that touch upon the sense of smell.

As you might guess, a very sensitive sense of smell is needed by anyone who seeks to enter this profession. In addition, a strong enthusiasm is required, since you must learn the qualities of thousands of raw and synthetic substances that are used to concoct scents. Carlos Benaim, senior perfumer for International Flavors and Fragrances, Inc., one of the industry's largest firms, said that it usually takes five years of laboratory experience apprenticing under a senior perfumer for a man or woman to gain competency in the field. Since there are no schools in this country that teach the art, laboratory apprenticing is the usual route of entry. A chemistry background is very helpful, but more important is a keen sense of smell.

Novice perfumers spend their time weighing and analyzing substances, testing for quality control, and performing routine laboratory chores. All the while they are studying the effects that certain substances have on the skin, how long scents linger, and the chemical properties of the scents themselves.

Finally, in the words of Mr. Benaim, a perfumer can "take combinations of ingredients that represent a certain note and use them to compose harmonies and choruses of scent."

In the path that leads up to this rarefied atmosphere of competence, a perfumer would start by earning between $300 and $400 per week in laboratory work. Senior perfumers earn a significant amount more, especially if they can sniff out new trends. The industry is centered around New York City and Paris, and there are 20 major firms and scores of smaller ones. The New York Business-to-Business Yellow Pages has a large listing of perfume manufacturers and is an excellent source to begin nosing through for leads.

52 Pet Cemetery Owner

A simple memorial stone at a pet cemetery reads, "Tiger, a good cat and a good friend." In death, Tiger received the dignity that is accorded to a loved one. In essence, that dignity is what pet cemeteries are all about.

There are several hundred pet cemeteries around the country, and their numbers will be growing as more people are turning to animals to fill the emotional need for companionship. Wendell C. Morse, director of the International Association of Pet Cemeteries, said that a person who seeks to establish a pet cemetery should plan on setting aside at least five acres of land. In California, New Jersey, and Ohio, this acreage must be dedicated and used as such in perpetuity. The legal requirements and guidelines are available by writing to the:

International Association of Pet Cemeteries
P.O. Box 1346
South Bend, IN 46624

In general, a pet cemetery is best located in an area near a major urban center. Town zoning ordinances must be considered as well as future development plans based on housing and business needs. The plot size for each grave is typically two feet by four feet. The price for such a plot varies, and depends on whether there is simply a flat burial fee or a yearly maintenance charge. Pet cemetery owners also have the opportunity to establish a concession that sells pet coffins and tombstones. Morse said that birds and reptiles are sometimes buried, but dogs and cats predominate.

As for pet cemetery owners, Morse said many deeply love animals and also seek to own a business that is a little different. They must have a sense of compassion because the loss of a pet is an emotional blow to many people. As Morse explained, "In many cases a pet becomes the central part of a person's life."

53 Piano Tuner

"Piano tuners use a tine to tune"–saying this three times fast may trip the tongue, but it may also provide basic understanding of the piano tuner's craft.

Whoever invented the piano was a craftsman and a genius. In the hands of a gifted pianist, this instrument produces some of the most beautiful sounds imaginable–its beauty being contained in the complexity of the overtones.

As with most musical instruments, the piano requires regular maintenance and upkeep. Tuning a piano is not a do-it-yourself job, however, and this is where piano tuners come in to play, for their abilities ensure that the instrument is at peak performance. A list of schools teaching the craft of piano tuning is available from the:

Piano Technicians Guild, Inc.
9140 Ward Parkway
Kansas City, MO 64114

Courses at the schools cover the mechanics of pianos, properties of acoustics, and tuning procedures. The most important part of the training is devoted to learning the sound of a correctly tuned piano. Perfect pitch is not necessary, according to Charles Huether, past president of the Guild. Instead, Huether said, an individual must "practice and cultivate hearing as a skill."

A trained ear is the most important "tool" that a

tuner can have. There are devices on the market that electronically measure pitch, but many tuners still rely on using an "A" tuning fork. The tuner sounds the "A" and compares it to the equivalent key on the piano. Once the two match, all other keys are corrected to this reference tone. A tuner adjusts harmonic intervals by hitting the key with one hand and adjusting the tuning pin with a specially constructed hammer. Other parts of the piano that need adjusting include the foot pedals and the felt pads that actually strike the note. Since each of the 230 strings in a grand piano need to be tuned individually, patience must be a key part of a tuner's character.

Most piano tuners enjoy being independently employed, although some spend their initial years after school apprenticing to an experienced tuner. In addition to tuning in homes, piano tuners contract with schools and music conservatories to tune their pianos. A piano is affected by seasonal changes and it usually needs tuning twice a year, although a concert piano will be tuned for each performance. If repair work or major adjustments are not needed, a piano tuner averages between $25 and $75 per job, depending on the region of the country in which he or she resides.

Due to the independent nature of the work, Huether said, piano tuners need to be self-starters. A love of music helps as does personal satisfaction in contributing to a musician's efforts. Huether summed it up by saying, "Piano tuners are a necessary part of an endeavor that helps to make life worth living."

54 Pipe Maker

A pipe is more than a mere smoking instrument. Stem turned outward, it is an effective pointer. Lightly rapped on a table, it can command attention. And gazed at as it emits a wraith of scented smoke, it can become a focal point of meditation. Indeed, a good pipe is a close friend. Pipe smokers who understand this latter statement appreciate the design and quality of a fine handmade pipe, and fortunately, there are artisans who can make their "pipe dreams" come true.

Mark Tinsky of the American Smoking Pipe Company, said that pipe makers first of all enjoy smoking themselves. Many start making pipes as a hobby, carving them from blocks of briar wood (the preferred pipe-making material), and gradually teach themselves the craft. Tinsky said that both a sense of design and woodworking skills are necessary to achieve artistry in pipe making. Both hand and power tools are used to fashion pipes and Tinsky said a pipe can take anywhere from several hours to a week to complete, depending on the pipe maker's skill and the intricacy of the design.

Tinsky noted that avid pipe smokers need seven to eight pipes in their collection so as to allow each pipe to "rest" and dry out between uses. Although machine-tooled pipes are available, a handmade model adds mystique to the whole activity, even though such a pipe may cost between $30 and $100. Pipe makers have two major ways of reaching their customers. The first is to wholesale to tobacco stores. This involves selling and merchandising skills. A second route is via direct sales (you can exhibit your wares at flea markets and craft fairs or sell by mail order), which eliminates retail middlemen. Tinsky said you must choose one way or the other, since stores won't carry your pipes if you are also selling them directly.

If you are interested in exploring the craft of pipe making, purchase pre-drilled blocks of briar wood from the:

American Smoking Pipe Company
P.O. Box 1298
Stroudsburg, PA 18360

Then see if your business really catches fire.

55 Polygrapher

A polygraph operator can help determine the answer to one of life's most profound mysteries–is the check REALLY in the mail? Commonly known as a "lie detector," the polygraph is an instrument that detects the slight changes in body functions that signal an emotional reaction. According to the American Polygraph Association, a person cannot avoid an emotional response when telling a falsehood.

A polygrapher should be an even-tempered, mild-mannered college graduate with an interest in the field of criminal justice, according to polygrapher Richard Humber of the firm of John Reed and Associates in Chicago. Training takes place at one of the 28 government and private schools around the country (the federal government maintains its own facilities to train polygraphers for security clearance work). Courses range from eight weeks to six months long, during which time a polygrapher studies psychology, physiology, pharmacology, and instrumentation. The polygraph itself is a suitcase-sized machine with wires attached to sensors. The sensors measure changes in such functions as perspiration and pulse, and a polygrapher notes the different peaks and valleys that are charted when questions are asked. Obviously truthful answers to questions such as name and age constitute the benchmark against which later responses are judged. Polygraphers are trained not to ask leading or ambivalent questions.

Upon completion of training, a polygrapher usually

must complete an internship. Complete information about state licensing requirements and accredited schools is available from the:

American Polygraph Association
Suite 408
Osborne Office Center
Chattanooga, TN 37411

Polygraphers earn from $18,000 to $22,000 per year. Clients include retail firms and institutions where large volumes of money are handled, such as banks. A polygrapher cannot prevent employee theft, but can help to promote the idea that honesty is the best policy.

56 Powderman

A powderman is an individual who gets a charge out of his work. Wherever there is building, tunneling, or mining activity, skilled demolition people will always be needed.

A powderman (also known as a blaster) usually goes through an apprenticeship program with the firm for which he works. Prior experience, such as military demolition work, may not count since firms usually like to train their people from the beginning. An apprentice blaster will learn charge size, rock types, and where to effectively place explosives along fault lines. It will take at least six months to learn the basics, which include "Do's and Don'ts," a formalized checklist for safety that is standardized throughout the industry. An advanced course in explosive technology, offered by DuPont Chemical of Wilmington, Delaware, may also be included in the training sequence. Due to the nature of the work, this profession calls for level-headed people with plenty of common sense and a strong regard for safety. The ability to follow explicit instructions to the letter is also required, again due to the premium put on safe procedures.

When your training is complete, you must be licensed by the state fire marshal and sign affidavits stating that you have never had a felony conviction and that you are not a drug or alcohol abuser. Powdermen are paid between $12 and $17 per hour. Once you're involved with blasting, the learning never stops. A blaster is always confronting new challenges in the career of making molehills out of mountains.

57 Presidential Advance Person

The phrase "the campaign trail" takes on a special meaning for the several hundred advance people who live out of suitcases for months on end as they criss-cross the country like long-haul truckers to direct the traveling road show of a presidential campaign.

Advance people live by the motto "Everything will be just fine." They enter a city anywhere from two to ten days before the arrival of the candidate and secure the beachheads by seeing to such details as the seating priority for local politicians, contacting local campaign organizations, organizing motorcades, seeing to hotel reservations, drumming up constituent support, and somewhere, somehow, trying to get their laundry done. As one advance manual succinctly put it, "Be tireless, sleep after the visit."

There are usually two to five people who compose an advance team. They can range from college students who have taken a semester off from school to seasoned pros in their forties or fifties who have advanced several campaigns. All must be diplomats, for the business of politics is, more than anything, the business of harnessing egos and ambitions to achieve a common goal.

Negotiating ability, tact, and above all, calmness under pressure will help you pave the way for a successful visit that photographs well for the evening news. They will also help you prevent the gaffes and fi-

119

ascoes that also photograph well for the evening news, and often spell the instant demise of an advance's career, not to mention the candidate's hopes.

Being an advance for either major party is a hectic job with no real security, but for those who have a taste for living on the cutting edge of history, it's a highly desirable position, for which there is no lack of hopefuls. There are several ways to ease into the job, all needing a fair amount of luck.

The maneuverings for a presidential campaign usually start two years before the election. You have to read the winds and see who is likely to commit to the race. Approach the potential candidate through a letter or interview and volunteer your services, especially in the area of organizing fund-raising appearances. As momentum builds, so could your duties.

Dovetailing into this method is the tried and true route of personal contacts. Do you know someone who can perform introductions? You cannot be bashful in this business. Field promotions are another possibility. Local organizers who deliver outstanding performances can catch the eye of the national staff. A few well-placed recommendations and a rally organizer might wind up traveling full time.

Working six months every four years for $100 per day plus expenses might seem a meager way of earning a living, but there is the possibility that your efforts will be handsomely rewarded. A president-elect obviously needs a staff. Even if a job in Washington does not materialize, you will end up with a nationwide network of friends and contacts with whom to swap beers and war stories.

58 Private Investigator

Back in the days when Sherlock Holmes donned his disguises and trailed transgressors through the foggy streets of London, anyone with the skills and the desire could open shop as a private investigator. Although the laws concerning invasions of privacy have somewhat modified the scope of present-day private eye (PI) activities, the mission is still the same–the gathering of information in a discreet and timely fashion.

The three areas that investigators typically work in are civil, criminal, and personal matters. Clients frequently include law firms and insurance companies–both of whom depend on private eyes to locate witnesses and secure evidence that is necessary to support their cases.

Governmental agencies on the federal, state, and county levels rely on investigative firms to conduct background checks of prospective employees. An increasing number of corporations are retaining investigators to uncover theft, industrial espionage, and white-collar crimes such as money laundering. These are bread-and-butter jobs for investigators, the regular contracts that help pay the bills. The side of the business that interests television involves cases where PIs are retained to pursue a variety of personal causes, such as finding Maltese falcons or digging up dirt for a divorce suit.

Besides feeling comfortable in rental cars and wigs, a good investigator needs to develop skills related to

121

the objective of getting information from a variety of sources as smoothly as possible. At all times you should constantly be expanding a circle of confidants, because you never know when a court clerk in Butte, Montana, or a newspaper reporter in Oakland, California, might come in handy. Helpful backgrounds for this profession include jobs involving research or interviewing, especially journalism and investigative reporting. Debt collectors, law enforcement personnel, and military investigators adapt quite well to the field. Women have an advantage, according to investigator Mary Ellen McWilliams of Virginia, since "nobody ever expects them to be getting information."

The regulation of the profession varies greatly from state to state. Most require that a person first work for a licensed agency. Such firms may be found via the Yellow Pages of a telephone book. Depending on aptitude, an investigator can earn between $7.50 and $12 per hour. To start your own business you will usually need a police background check, a surety bond or professional liability insurance, a business license, and in some states such as Virginia, formal classroom study and seminars on law and police procedures.

The rate you command as an independent private investigator depends in part on experience and reputation, and on geographic locale. In most metropolitan areas, agencies charge between $25 and $100 per hour, plus expenses. Investigators usually receive a retainer based on the number of hours the case is expected to entail. Final billing is completed when the client receives a comprehensive written report.

The glamor that is associated with the profession is just as well left on the television screen. Private eyes spend countless hours doing tedious searches of records, interviewing recalcitrant witnesses, and calling individuals on the telephone. Stale leads and blind alleys are all in a day's work. But the lead that works sets you up for the thrill of the chase, a thrill that Sherlock Holmes knew quite well.

59 Professional Diver

Underwater adventure did not end when the television show "Seahunt" left the airwaves. If anything, the demand for professional divers is increasing, as advanced technology makes the depths of the ocean more accessible. The options open to divers are varied, potentially dangerous, and profitable. Divers earn a living searching for sunken treasure, performing underwater construction, and collecting exotic tropical fish, in addition to teaching courses in scuba diving at swimming pools across the country.

If you want to learn the skills involved with underwater construction, then the first step is to contact a member school of the:

Association of Commercial Diving Educators
c/o Professional Diving School of New York
222 Fordham Street
City Island, NY 10464

Glenn Butler, who is with the New York school, said a person should be a high school graduate, scuba-certified, and mechanically inclined. A stint with the military is also a plus. After you have been accepted, you will undergo a six-month training period that covers the physics of diving, equipment use and repair, and safety procedures. Heavy emphasis is placed on the latter because of the obvious danger involved in this profession. Students learn underwater welding, blasting, salvage, search and recover, and television camera technique. Related courses include working with small, manned submersibles and underwater vehicles. Upon graduation, divers can either freelance or become salaried divers for firms involved with oil, construction, maintenance, or salvage work. The salary scale reflects the hazardous nature of the work, and Butler said divers can earn between $25,000 and $100,000 per year. He also noted that many divers work well into their 60s since their experience is invaluable.

Another slant on the profession is offered by firms such as Exotix International in Islamorada, Florida. Exotix buys tropical fish and other marine creatures from divers who collect the animals from reefs along the Florida coast and the Keys. The wildlife is then sold to zoos and pet shops. Exotix owner Dave Hill said divers earn between 50 cents and $5 per fish netted, so you can average $100 per day for your efforts. Since the work is strictly freelance, you must have your own equipment and boat. Hill said anyone can engage in collection work, but that skill and efficiency only come with experience. Hill said that dive shops are good places to find out who in the area buys fish. "When you enjoy diving in the first place," he observed, "it's a good way to earn a living."

60 Professional Wrestler

The antics that one sees at a professional wrestling match often resemble a Marx Brothers' version of a sumo wrestling tournament. The costumes, stage personas, and ring theatrics are designed purely for entertainment, but still, there is much more to the sport. The men and women who perform as professional wrestlers are highly trained athletes who can stand a good deal of physical mayhem.

To become a professional wrestler, you should be in your late teens or early twenties. Good starting weights are 220 to 225 pounds for men and 120 to 130 pounds for women. You should also be in excellent physical shape, according to Charley Fulton, a wrestling coach at the Monster Factory, a premier gym for training wrestlers. The address of the gym is:

Monster Factory
P.O. Box 345
Westville, NJ 08093

Upon entering a training program, Fulton said, you should expect to train four to five months to learn the various holds and counterholds in the sport. "We first start with teaching people how to fall correctly. It's the most important thing to know," Fulton said.

While undergoing training, a novice also develops a wrestling personality, the "good guy" or "bad guy" image that wrestling crowds love. Towards the end of their training, wrestlers start to meet with various wrestling show promoters, or a videotape of the wrestler in action is sent to booking agencies.

Once on the circuit, which can include small town high school auditoriums or big city arenas, a wrestler can work up to five or six nights a week, fighting a 20- to 60-minute match each night. Fulton estimated that a starting wrestler can earn between $20,000 and $30,000 per year, out of which traveling expenses must be paid. Once a wrestler gets experience and connects with the World Wrestling Federation, it is possible to earn up to about $100,000 per year.

However, this is a profession in which your education will include a few hard knocks. The risk of physical injury is always present and most wrestlers phase out of the sport by their late thirties because of that. Also, due to the ego of some individual wrestlers, it may be difficult to develop friendships with other athletes. "There are a lot of wrestlers who just don't care for each other," Fulton said.

Those who become wrestlers obviously enjoy physical contact sports. In addition to earnings, they also relish the chance to be "ringed" by crowds of cheering spectators.

61 Prospector

If you have gold fever, the only known antidote is a cold mountain stream and a panful of gravel. The actual cure of finding a gold nugget may take a while, and it usually brings on a recurrence of the original malady.

With the high price that gold is now commanding, the gold rush is returning to many small mining communities, only now four-wheel drive vehicles and portable dredges have largely replaced burros and pick axes. There are two ways to recover gold: mine it from a lode, or dredge it from a stream. Mining involves the filing of claims and environmental impact statements, followed by blasting the rock, crushing it, and then leaching the gold out with acid. It involves a lot of hard, dirty work, but it can pay off with spectacular results if a rich vein is struck. Dredging involves scooping up gravel from a river bottom with a portable dredge and washing the rock through a sluice box to recover the gold that has found its way to the river bottom from eroded mineral-bearing rock in the mountains. Needless to say, both mining and dredging involve luck.

Steve Teter of the Gold Prospectors of America says there is still a lot of gold in them thar hills, since each spring more rock is washed away from the mountainsides. The major states where prospecting is taking place are Alaska, California, Oregon, and Arizona. "If there was gold in the area before, there is gold there now," Teter said.

You can buy the necessary equipment (pan, sluice

box, and dredge) for under $500. Owing to the nature of the work, you may or may not reclaim this investment. The trick is to determine if a site looks promising so as not to waste time and effort dredging up worthless rock. To that extent, Teter suggested that amateurs who are serious about prospecting should learn the techniques by joining clubs that focus on gold prospecting. Clubs can be located through the:

Gold Prospectors Association of America
205 North Main Street
Fallbrook, CA 92028

The Association publishes a magazine, *Gold Prospector*, that has many helpful pointers

In addition to doing historic and geologic research on an area, you should contact local landowners or county and federal parks departments before dredging a stream. Although public lands are open for this type of activity, there may be seasonal restrictions that limit dredging to avoid interfering with fish spawning.

Once the gold is recovered, Teter said, it can be refined and sold on the spot market, or you can use it to fashion jewelry, often earning up to 10 times the spot price in the process. Prospectors who do well tend to be a bit close-mouthed about specific sites. They also love working in the outdoors and don't discourage easily. It often takes years to become a flash in the pan success.

62 Prosthetist/Orthotist

Artificial limb design has come a long way since the days of the proverbial peg-legged pirate. Sophisticated materials, electronic sensing devices, and other biomedical advances are providing amputees with a great deal of freedom and control in their lives.

Helping to pioneer these improvements are certified prosthetic (artificial limbs) and orthotic (braces) specialists. To get into this field, you need a bachelor's degree in a health or life science field. From there, you go on to take graduate work at a school that has a special program in these fields. A list of such schools is available from the:

American Board for the Certification of Orthotics and Prosthetics
717 Pendleton Street
Alexandria, VA 22314

A one- or two-year internship then follows, and upon its successful completion, you can take the necessary certifying exams.

Prosthetists (orthotists are very similar) work closely with doctors and physical therapists in assisting a patient's recovery. They are responsible for measuring and designing the artificial limbs that will connect to muscle and nerve groups in a patient's extremities. Each person must be fitted individually. There are no "off-the-shelf" devices. Once a limb is designed, technicians then fabricate the necessary parts. Starting salary for a prosthetist is around $20,000, which increases as one gains experience and competence. Certified prosthetists work at hospitals, own their own businesses, or are affiliated with existing prosthetic firms. It is interesting to note that many amputees have become involved with this profession.

Kirk Lucyk, a prosthetist with the firm of J.E. Hanger, said that it is necessary for people in the field to keep abreast of changing technology, so education is a continual process. As to the nonintrinsic rewards of the profession, Lucyk said,"I feel a sense of personal freedom by helping other people become independent again."

If you are interested in the actual fabrication of mechanical limbs and braces, there are several two-year programs available to high school graduates. They are:

Northeast Metro Technical Institute
3300 Central Avenue North
White Bear Lake, MN 55110

Spokane Falls Community College
Orthotics and Prosthetics Program
W3140 Ft. George Wright Drive MS-3060
Spokane, WA 99204-5288

Orthotics Technicians Program
Harmerville Rehabilitation Center
P.O. Box 11386
620 Alpha Drive
Pittsburgh, PA 15238-0386

63 Pyrotechnist

The artistry of a fireworks display leaves many spectators with the thought, "Gee, wouldn't it be fun to set those off!" Well, it is fun for the men and women who light up the night as fireworks pyrotechnists. In fact, they get a bang out of their job.

To be a successful pyrotechnician, you cannot have a short fuse. Maturity and common sense are critical when working around explosive material. In some states pyrotechnists must be licensed by the state fire marshal. Pyrotechnists are hired by fireworks manufacturers to put on displays around the country. A team of two to four arrive at a site during the day to set up the mortars that lob the shells, and to construct any stationary displays that will be lit. At night, the fireworks are detonated either manually or electronically following a choreographed script.

John Leonard, past president of the Pyrotechnics Guild, said it takes at least 30 to 40 shows before a person is proficient enough to go out on their own. A pyrotechnician, he said, is concerned with both safety and showmanship. There is a great deal of responsibility involved, since the chief pyrotechnician has the authority to cancel a show if weather or wind conditions appear unfavorable.

George Zambelli, president of the internationally known Zambelli Internationale Fireworks, said his company uses pyrotechnists who live in various parts of the country to shoot off their displays. He said Zambelli Internationale looks for people who love to be entertainers and who are willing to dedicate themselves to mastering the craft. Training is provided for novices at the firm's headquarters in New Castle, Pennsylvania.

Leonard said there is keen competition among fireworks firms to hire away competent pyrotechnists. As for salary, individuals receive about $150 per show for smaller displays or a percentage of the gross on larger shows. Leonard suggested that anyone interested in the field contact the:

> **Pyrotechnics Guild**
> c/o John Leonard
> 8841 Satyr Hill Road
> Baltimore, MD 21234

As long as people *ohh* and *ahh* over fireworks, there will always be a need for pyrotechnists. It is a profession that will never go up in smoke.

64 Racetrack Announcer

"And they're off . . . coming into the far stretch, it's Lunch Hour leading at 12 to 1 . . ." Thus could start another day in the life of a racetrack announcer. Perched high above the track, his keen eye and accurate recital keep railbirds informed as to whether they should head towards the payoff window or to the exit door.

Track announcers should love the sport of horseracing, according to Tom Cosentino, publicity director for Yonkers Raceway in New York. "Anybody can try it, there are no restrictions and you don't necessarily need a great voice," he said. What you do need is an accurate memory, since an announcer must memorize the jockeys' colors before the race and be able to chart the progress of the horses by spotting the colors.

Most track announcers start by practicing on their own. They come to the track with a pair of binoculars and a tape recorder and call race after race until they get proficient enough to send off demonstration tapes to various raceways. "You start with the smaller tracks to build your experience and add color to your style. Then you graduate to being a backup announcer at a larger track, and finally you become the main announcer," Cosentino said. Track announcers can earn over $100 per day, but they have to work long hours when calling 10 to 11 races per day. But, as Cosentino said, "If you're going to be at the racetrack anyway, you might as well give it a shot."

65 Raft Guide

In whitewater rafting, the journey is more important than the destination. Due to an increased awareness of the outdoors, Americans are taking to whitewater rafting in ever-increasing numbers. On the East Coast there are 22 major and numerous minor rivers that can be rafted, and in the West, serious rafters tackle just about any moving waterway, including rivers along the Rocky and Cascade ranges.

People who are devoted to rafting will have their own inflatable equipment and indulge in the sport on their own, but those who raft only occasionally or are new to it generally do it through outfitting companies. In order to protect both their investment and the lives of customers, these companies use river guides familiar with both raft handling and the intricacies of white water.

Mike Rock of Eastern River Expeditions in Maryland said that men and women who act as guides know about being very wet and very cold. "There are definitely good days and bad days on the river," he noted.

Guides usually are trained in early spring before the start of the recreation season. They learn to navigate the branches of the rivers that they will be working on, noting currents, eddies, and rocks. They also learn how to unpin rafts, throw ropes, and handle launchings. The actual raft trip can take anywhere from several hours to a few days. At the conclusion, the rafts and rafters return by bus or truck to the point of embarkation.

Rock said those who do well as raft guides love the outdoors and like to work with people. Other skills that are helpful are in the area of emergency medical training. You can enter the profession in several ways. The first is through recommendations of existing guides. Another is to become so involved with the sport that you keep returning throughout the summer as a company's paying customer. Existing guides who notice this enthusiasm may then suggest that you apply for a full-time position. A third method is to take a professional guiding course offered by many companies. The courses can cost several hundred dollars, and there is no guarantee of a job when you complete the course. But many firms are now hiring only from the pool of individuals who have taken it.

Persons who are interested in locating outfitting companies can do so through any of the following:

Eastern Professional River Outfitters Association
530 South Gay Street, Suite 222
Knoxville, TN 37902

Western River Guides Association
7600 East Arapahoe Road
Englewood, CO 80112

American Whitewater Affiliation
146 North Brockway
Palatine, IL 60067

The latter group puts out an informative publication called *American Whitewater*. Another source of excellent all-round information is the book *Wild Rivers of North America*, by Michael Jenkinson, which can be obtained from out-of-print bookstores.

The rafting season varies in different areas of the country since it depends on water temperature and river height. During the season a guide earns between $40 and $80 per day. Time not spent on the river is spent repairing and maintaining equipment. A fringe benefit of this job is that as a guide you get to wash your clothes on every trip!

66 Repo Man

Well, somebody has to do it.

The "it" in this case involves the repossessing of cars and the "somebody" is a "repo" man.

When a bank or finance company notifies a repossession company that a car loan has gone into default, the company sends a repo man to locate the car and he in turn either notifies a tow truck to haul the car to an impoundment lot or drives the car himself after starting it with a pass key. This seemingly straightforward process gets slightly complicated due to the fact that some people don't want to have their cars towed away. For that reason, repo men work strange hours and have to think fast on their feet.

Since evening hours are usually the busiest, the profession is hard on family life. As one repo man put it, "This is an aggravating business." Individuals are paid on a flat fee basis of about $100 per car, and one recovery per day is average. The attraction to this rather solitary profession comes from knowing that each day and case will be different. Most of the repo man's time is spent sitting behind the wheel of a car, not behind some desk.

67 Rockette

Forget the fact that they are beautiful–it's their legs that cause people's jaws to drop, legs that kick so high they often threaten to punch holes in the roof. These girls are showstoppers. They are the Rockettes.

As one of America's premier dance troupes, they have toured the world and are the annual attraction at the Radio City Music Hall's Christmas show in New York City. They are also very dedicated professionals who work long hours to achieve their precise, synchronized routines.

Rockette Director, Violet Holmes, said that most of her 36-member troupe (plus 3 replacements) are between 20 and 30 years in age, and must stand between 5' 5 1/2" and 5' 8 1/2" in their stocking feet. "Lots of those inches should be in the legs," she noted. Because of the technical nature of their choreography, Ms. Holmes said applicants should have advanced tap training and knowledge of ballet and jazz routines. At present, the Rockettes have a 20-week engagement calendar, during which time they receive the going American Guild of Variety Artists (AGVA) union wage scale.

During their off season, Ms. Holmes said Rockettes seek shorter performance gigs, but all the while they keep limber and in shape. This physical conditioning is important, since over the Christmas holidays they do four 90-minute shows per day, seven days per week. "A dancer can stay as a Rockette as long as she can do the work, and the girls usually know when it is time to leave," Ms. Holmes said. But it is not all work and no play. Ms. Holmes noted that the Rockettes are a very tight-knit group, functioning in many ways as a large extended family.

The "family" members come from all parts of the country. Ms. Holmes said that if you seek to become a Rockette, you should send a resume to

Ms. Violet Holmes
Radio City Music Hall
44 West 51st Street
New York, NY 10020

The resumes are kept on file for two years, and if there are any auditions during that period, *everybody* on the list is notified, no matter where they reside. So if a girl has got great gams and the talent to match, she can kick up a storm in New York City.

68 Saddlemaker

In the history of country-western music, there is nary a song written about a saddlemaker. Yet these are the folks who enable both cowboys and weekend equestrians to sit tall in the saddle.

Saddlemakers learn their trade by apprenticing to saddleshops (mostly located in western states) or by attending schools that teach the skill. Here are four:

Cordwainer School
Walsall, England
(specializes in English saddles)

Oklahoma State Technical College
Fourth and Mission Streets
Okmulgee, OK 74447

Texas State Technical Institute
P.O. Box 11155
Amarillo, TX 79111

Spokane Community College
North 1810 Green Street
Spokane, WA 99207

The actual construction of a saddle involves layering and stitching foam and leather over a wooden or plastic frame. Ron Freesman, of the Tack Room in Westport, Connecticut, said that it generally takes a week to make a Western saddle and two days to make an English saddle, depending on the amount of decorative finish work that is involved. A saddle can cost between $200 and $8,000 with $1,200 being the median price.

The same technical schools in the United States that teach saddlemaking also teach the related craft of bootmaking. Tooled leather boots range between $350 and $2,000 a pair.

Saddlemakers and bootmakers earn between $15,000 and $25,000, depending on geographic location and on whether they own their own shops or work for someone else. They should love working with leather and should be precise, accurate, and patient. There should be a continuing demand for saddlemakers as people continue to enjoy leisure riding. The horse-related industry as a whole totals $16.5 billion yearly, which means there will be happy trails for years to come.

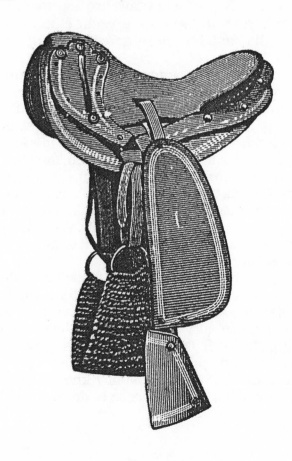

69 Sailmaker

Mainsail, foresail . . . these are terms that weekend sailors know by heart, and the word they have in common is "sail." A good set of sails are necessary for skippers and crews to "sew up" a yacht club victory. The people who fashion these acres of fabric are sailmakers.

Sailmaking shops, known as lofts, are found in all major centers of sailing activity. The lofts are vast open areas upon which sails are laid out for cutting and trimming. The sailmakers fashioning these sails are individuals who have both sewing skills and a knowledge of sailing. According to Walter Scanlon, foreman at Hild Sails in New York City, most sailmakers learn their craft on the job. "A person who sews well can start right away at the machine. Within a month's time he or she will know how to sew or finish sails. A cutter will take about one year to learn the different anglings and cuts for the sails," he said.

Scanlon said the salary scale for sailmakers ranges between $5 and $10 per hour, and that, aside from a few cuts from scissors there are no hazards, and you work in a clean, airy environment. A key advantage of learning the craft is that it transfers easily between shops. Scanlon added that after three to five years in the business, sailmakers usually know enough to set up their own loft if they choose to do so.

70 Shepherd

With all the talk today about high-tech jobs, it is refreshing to note the existence of a few no-tech careers, fields where a bit is something you put in a horse's mouth and a bite is something you take out of a sandwich. Shepherding is one of them.

The job description for this profession has not changed in the last several millennia. Shepherds are responsible for protecting their flocks from predators and guiding them to rich pastures to fatten for market.

Modern-day shepherds handle flocks of up to 1,400 sheep. These sheep usually spend the summer months grazing the mountain pastures of federal range land in the West. Each day, the shepherd must saddle up before sunrise to move the flock to fresh pasture. Sheep dogs such as border collies and shelties assist in herding the sheep. When a new grazing spot is reached, the shepherd breaks the flock into smaller bands so that they will not crowd each other while grazing.

During the day, the shepherd keeps an eye on the flock to prevent strays. At nightfall, the shepherd and the dogs gather the flock into a tight band for protection. Dawn and dusk are problem times for a shepherd, since this is when coyotes and other predators are likely to attack.

After the flock is bedded down, the shepherd retires to a simple covered wagon for an evening meal. Such tasty entrees as canned corn and beans are usually on the menu since the cramped quarters do not allow for refrigeration. A shepherd's job is never done, for even at night, the bark of a sheep dog or rumble of thunder may signify a problem demanding instant attention.

While in the mountains, a shepherd can earn between $500 and $750 a month plus provisions. The season lasts from early spring, when the sheep first go to high pastures, until the fall, when they return to the home ranch. Some shepherds are kept on through the winter to assist with feeding, lambing, or shearing chores.

This is certainly not the job for someone who enjoys life in the fast lane. The ranches and pastures are miles away from even a mile post, and a dog literally becomes man's best friend. But the solitude of mountain pastures and the bracing, pure, clean air are rewards enough for those who can appreciate nature's beauty.

Perhaps it is due to the remoteness, perhaps it is due to the long hours, but in any case, Bob Gilbert of the Montana Sheep Growers Association maintains "It's almost impossible to find good shepherds." Although American citizens are given preference, sheep ranchers often have to hire Peruvians and Basques because of the lack of qualified native-born applicants. Few ranchers are willing to immediately hand over $100,000 worth of sheep to a tenderfoot.

Gilbert suggests that if you want to become a shepherd you write the National Wool Growers Association and ask to be put in contact with the state organizations. The national association can be reached at the:

National Wool Growers Association
1301 Pennsylvania Avenue NW, Suite 300
Washington, DC 20004

The state groups in turn could help you locate a rancher who may need extra hands during the lambing season. This will give the rancher an opportunity to see how you work, and at the same time, you can discover if you're cut out to handle a life that truly follows a different bleat.

71 Smoke Jumper

A smoke jumper knows the meaning of the phrase "jumping from the frying pan into the fire."

Teams of smoke jumpers will circle a raging forest fire in small planes, then parachute into wooded areas to mount first-strike containment efforts against shifts in the blaze. Because of the treacherous terrain and shifting winds, several jumpers a year wind up with broken limbs. They also wind up with a fair share of stories to tell their grandchildren.

Smoke jumping is certainly not the easiest calling in the world. To even be considered as a smoke jumper, you must first spend at least two years fighting fires as a forestry technician, and you must be in top physical condition. Employment information about this position can be obtained from the:

U.S. Department of Agriculture
Forest Service
12th and Independence Avenue SW
P.O. Box 2417
Washington, DC 20013

After two seasons and with good recommendations from your fire bosses, you can then apply for a position as smoke jumper by again writing to the above address. Those selected are put through a six-week program that includes seven practice jumps and further fire fighting training.

Smoke jumpers may need to parachute up to 15 times per fire season. At a forest fire, the tools and equipment are parachuted out first. Smoke jumpers follow and begin their urgent work. Eventually they will be relieved by ground crews at which point they await their next jump assignments.

When they are not airborne, jumpers maintain a rigorous physical conditioning program. For their efforts smoke jumpers receive a salary of $18,300 per year. Some 40 openings occur each year. Those who fill them know that when their jobs are on the line, it means the fire line.

72 Square Dance Caller

It takes more than a "la-di-da" for a person to "do-si-do" into the role of a professional square dance caller. Callers are the central hub around which square dancers wheel through intricate designs. Their talents are honed by years of practice in both dancing and calling.

You can learn to be a square dance caller either through apprenticeship or by attending a "caller's college." If you choose the apprenticeship route, there are 7,000 active clubs comprising three million active dancers in the United States with which you can affiliate. A complete list of clubs can be found in the:

Square Dance Directory
P.O. Box 54055
Jackson, MS 39208

Keep contacting clubs until you find a caller willing to teach you, and train under his or her tutelage for several years.

If you plan to attend a caller's college, you should have at least two years of dancing experience. "A caller needs to know how to move and what moves are possible in combination," according to Stan Burdick, editor of the magazine *American Square Dancer*. Ads for colleges are contained in the publication, which can be ordered from

American Square Dancer
P.O. Box 488
Huron, Oh 44839

Classes last from three days to one week, during which time callers learn microphone skills, how to compose patterns extemporaneously, and how to handle large crowds of dancers. Burdick said good callers should love dancing, and have good diction, a good singing voice, and a thorough knowledge of the scores of moves that lead to a smooth-flowing dance.

Callers earn $50 to $100 per night. Many start their careers by teaching adult education courses in square dancing and then forming clubs from the graduates.

Another popular style of recreational dance is international folk dancing. Folk dance teachers learn their skills at a variety of workshops and camps. Some teachers specialize in dances from a particular ethnic group while others master a wide range of dances. Dance teachers charge varying fees for their services. Some are employed by adult education departments and others establish their own studios. Here are two good sources of folk dance information:

People's Folk Dance Directory
P.O. Box 8575
Austin, TX 78713

Folk Dance House
P.O. Box 2305
North Babylon, NY 11703

The latter is particularly useful in learning about courses that occur on short notice. By becoming involved in either folk or square dancing, you can combine recreation with an income. It thus affords you the opportunity to dance through life.

73 Stained Glass Artisan

Stained glass windows and churches have a natural affinity for each other. Their radiant hues appear to please both body and soul. The people who make them possible are stained glass artisans.

These men and women learn their skill by taking classes and apprenticing at stained glass firms. To do this work, you must have an accurate eye and a steady hand, since the glass is cut from a full-sized pattern and then inserted into leaded strips called canes. It usually takes three to five years to learn the craft, and an experienced artisan earns between $10 and $12 per hour. The potential of creating a work of great beauty is balanced by working conditions that require caution. Constant contact with glass dust, lead, and hydrochloric acid are health hazards that you must bear in mind. If you are interested in becoming an artisan, the best place to find a local firm specializing in stained glass is through the telephone book Yellow Pages.

Stained glass designing is another pane of the profession. These artists are usually people with a formal art background who enjoy the medium of stained glass and are also familiar with its limitations. Not all paintings, for instance, will transfer easily to glass windows. Designers are either commissioned directly by churches, businesses, or private parties or are retained by stained glass firms to do design work for them.

74 Stamp Designer

Some folks are stuck on stamps. A spiffy commemorative is to them much more than merely a way of getting mail delivered. It's a way of adding pizazz to the otherwise mundane activity of sending a letter. To cater to this large body of stamp lovers, the U.S. Post Office promotes a stamp program that features an extensive range of commemorative issues. Famous people, historical events, and topical themes have all been incorporated into stamp designs.

Making all of these miniature works of art possible are freelance stamp designers who are selected by the Citizen Stamp Advisory committee, a 15-member volunteer panel that meets six times a year. This panel is responsible for recommending subjects and designs for the approval of the postmaster-general.

The committee gets advice from professional designers who are under contract to the Post Office. Once a theme has been decided upon, the designers review the work of available artists and recommend three whose work might be suitable for the stamp under consideration. The artists are selected from previous stamp designers, peers of the design coordinators, or from those artists who submit resumes and up to three publication tear sheets (no original artwork) to the following address:

Stamp Information Branch
Post Office Headquarters
Room 5800
Washington, DC 20260

This material is kept in a design file, and philatelic program specialist Hugh McGonigle said there is an effort each year to see that at least one-third of the stamps are done by new designers in order to keep the drawings fresh.

Once the three artists are approved by the committee, the coordinators aid them by supplying technical guidance on design and production. The artists have up to 60 days to complete their work, and although only one sketch is accepted, each artist receives a fee of $3,000. It would then be another two years before the stamp is released, thus allowing time for printing, perforating, and shipping. McGonigle said the artist is invited to the first-day-of-issue ceremonies, thus allowing an admiring public to put its stamp of approval on his or her work.

75 Steeplejack

This profession allows you to get to the top fast–but not by climbing a corporate ladder. Steeplejacks are proud craftsmen whose demanding profession requires that they ascend to heights up to 1,000 feet to refurbish or repair radio towers, church steeples, and any other structure that architects choose to build to the heavens.

As you might guess, the prime requirement for a steeplejack is a healthy respect for heights. A beginning steeplejack spends the first few weeks on the ground. This time is spent learning and honing skills related to carpentry, masonry, steel work, painting, and gold leaf application. This ground training is important, since a job done correctly on the ground can save costly hours in the air.

But a beginning steeplejack soon gets a chance to be airborne. "I like to see early in the game whether a man likes to climb or not," said Steve Quinn of Skyline Engineers of Fitchburg, Massachusetts. The steeplejack sits in a "bosun's chair" which is lowered to the worksite by ropes and pulleys. This precarious system eliminates the need for costly scaffolding at a job site.

Steeplejacks can spend up to several months on the road, and Quinn said this is usually hard for a married man with a family to handle. For those who are young and unattached, however, the excitement of climbing and the opportunity to travel are prime attractions.

The trade also attracts individuals with an innovative turn of mind, since each contract is different. You must be resourceful enough to be a jack of one trade and the master of many.

A profession closely related to the steeplejack's is that of being a skyscraper window washer. Window washers perform their task via scaffolding which is lowered from the top of a building or by climbing out of a window onto a ledge, hooking a safety belt onto a clamp, leaning back, and washing the window. "Most people do it for the money," said Joe Eitner, vice-president of operations for Supreme Building Maintenance in New York City. "A person can earn nearly $500 per week. They have to be self-motivated because there is nobody looking over their shoulder. It's high-risk, but not unsafe if a person uses his equipment correctly."

Union membership may or may not be required for window washers. Firms doing this work can be located via the Yellow Pages or by contacting the building maintenance department of large office skyscrapers.

Both window washers and steeplejacks are attracted to the high rewards that come with high risks. Theirs are professions where the sky is the limit.

76 Stone Carver

"There's a shape in that stone, no doubt about it. I just have to bring it out." Those words of Washington Cathedral stone carver Patrick Plunkett perfectly sum up a craft that has brought forth some of mankind's most magnificent structures. This is a proud profession, for the intricate detail work and impressive statuary that stone carvers create will last until stone weathers into dust. When a stone carver at the Washington Cathedral was asked why he spent so much time shaping a cornice that would be hidden several stories off the ground, his reply was simple–"Because God sees it."

A stone carver learns the craft by the traditional apprenticeship system. Male and female apprentices learn the use of mallets, chisels, and handheld pneumatic air hammers, as well as the characteristics of different types of stone. Master stone carvers first teach their students how to chisel and etch simple shapes, such as leaves and letters. As a student's technique improves and confidence increases, so does the difficulty of the assignment. Shapes and figures are explained, as are the techniques of working from scaffolding. Each person's training is individual because each person's talent is unique.

A stone carver need not have a right arm the size of a heavyweight boxer to be successful. The ability to draw and perceive forms, however, is necessary. There are several schools in the world that teach stone carving. In New York City, there is a four-year program associated with the St. John the Divine Cathedral. Apprentices earn about $10,000 per year, and the number of apprentices admitted each year depends on the funding the church receives. No prior experience is necessary, but prospective carvers must undergo a series of interviews and show a strong desire to commit themselves to be a stone carver. For more information contact the:

Stone Carving Program
St. John the Divine Cathedral
1047 Amsterdam Avenue
New York, NY 10025

The St. John's program is notable since it offers a nominal salary during the apprenticeship program. Those who successfully complete the course stay on as stone carvers at the cathedral. Other schools that teach stone carving are the Bath Technical College in Bath, England; the South Dorset Technical College in South Dorset, England; and the Pietra Santa in Carrara, Italy.

The salary for journeyman and master stone carvers varies according to ability and job site. A stone carver may spend an entire lifetime at one site, or may travel around the country doing restorative and decorative work on churches and public buildings. Plunkett said there will always be a demand for talented stone carvers. Once a person's credentials are established, advertising is not necessary–architects will come looking.

There is a good chance that during the course of a career, a stone carver can develop respiratory complications from rock dust, and there is a good chance that a stone carver will not live to see the end result of his or her artistry. Both the Washington Cathedral and St. John the Divine will take years to complete. But there is also a good chance that someone else will be marveling at their craftsmanship generations and generations and generations from now.

77 Surf Lifeguard

You don't have to be handsome or beautiful to be a surf lifeguard.

Only competent.

Hollywood has certainly glamorized the profession, but it takes more than a movie star to save a drowning person. Surf lifeguards are the premier individuals in the water safety profession and they perform their important duties at recreation beaches along the country's seacoasts. In many cases, they are employed by the parks and recreation departments of the cities or counties that administer the waterfronts. (You can locate the correct department by calling the city hall information number.) Such is the case with the San Diego City Lifeguard Service in California. Its requirements can be generalized for services around the country.

To be a surf lifeguard in San Diego, you must be at least 17 years old (the average age is 22), have a minimum eyesight of 20/40 corrected to 20/20, and must pass a physical test of running 50 meters, swimming 500 offshore meters, and running another 50 meters in less than 10 minutes. This qualifies you for an interview. "We basically are looking for an honest, responsible person, not someone who is out for the glamor," said lifeguard Robert Lange.

After being accepted as a lifeguard, you then undergo a week's training in rescue techniques, lifesaving equipment use, and emergency medical care. An extensive in-service training program is also conducted during the season.

Lange said that guards usually work staggered eight-hour shifts. An early morning guard may be responsible for several miles of beach. But as the crowds begin to gather, it is common for guards to be stationed in towers spaced every 300 yards.

The major problems that a lifeguard must deal with are poor swimmers and people who get caught by rip currents and unexpected dropoffs. Guards use buoys, rescue boards, and rubberized power boats to assist in rescues. "The dories are now mostly used for competition," Lange said. On shore, lifeguards perform a public relations function, helping mothers find their children, holding onto lost jewelry, etc.

Lange said that surf lifeguards are athletic, people-oriented individuals with a slant towards water sports such as scuba diving or surfing. For their efforts they receive between $7.50 and $12.50 per hour, depending on experience and length of service. In addition to the opportunity to work outdoors, lifeguards also enjoy a close-knit camaraderie based on mutual respect. "We're very proud of what we do," Lange said.

78 Symphony Conductor

A conductor in action is music in motion. A symphony-goer can literally see as well as hear a performance by watching a symphony conductor's broad sweeping arm movements and the short staccato hand choppings of the baton. But it takes more than just a waggling of the arms to become a symphony conductor. This is a profession that requires years of training and hard work.

Most conductors are accomplished musicians who pursued their studies with their instruments at one of the noted schools around the country. Advanced music courses then exposed them to conducting techniques. At some point they became more interested in conducting than in playing.

Upon graduating with a degree in conducting from a music school, a beginning conductor starts to establish his or her reputation via fellowships, internships, and guest appearances. The Boston Symphony, for instance, has an eight-week fellowship program which it holds each summer when it performs at the Tanglewood Music Center in western Massachusetts. Young conductors can learn from experienced masters while studying the theory and history of different compositions. To apply, contact the:

Program in Orchestral Conducting
Symphony Hall
Boston, MA 02115

The American Symphony Orchestra League, based

in Washington, D.C., also selects young conductors to perform at its annual convention in New York City. Over 800 orchestras belong to the league, and they all need conductors and assistant conductors. Many medium-sized cities look for young conductors to take charge of their programs.

"We recently hired a woman conductor with a vibrant personality. We consider ourselves a developing organization, and we look for conductors on the way up who are willing to take musicians and work with them," said Lawrence Moffat, president of the Johnson City (Tennessee) Symphony.

"A conductor has to work in seven clefs and also needs to know how to transpose music. You should never stop training in this profession. After 10 years a conductor should have 2,000 to 3,000 orchestral works in his or her repertoire," said Tom Corbett, assistant orchestra librarian at the Juilliard School in New York City.

A conductor who starts his or her career with a mid-sized symphony earns between $18,000 and $30,000 per year. A conductor with a major orchestra will earn upwards of six figures annually. The conductor may also double as music director and take on other tasks with the orchestra. An important factor is effective use of rehearsal time. Rehearsals are expensive, and it behooves a conductor to use them efficiently. A good conductor thus should manage as well as lead an orchestra.

Management, leadership, musical ability, showmanship–all of these talents are involved with the position of symphony conductor. The person who wields the conductor's baton uses the whole orchestra as an instrument.

79 Syndicated Columnist

If you doodle cartoons on a regular basis à la Gary Larson or have noticed that grass actually does grow greener over the septic tank à la Erma Bombeck, then perhaps it is time to gather together your ideas and get them before a national audience as a syndicated columnist or cartoonist.

It's not just "the other guy" who breaks into print in this fashion. A spokeswoman for the News-America Syndicate said, "We are looking for anything and everything." Material can be sent to the:

Syndication Manager
News-America Syndicate
1703 Kaiser Avenue
Irvine, CA 92664

Other syndication services can be found in *Literary Market Place* or the *Syndicated Columnist Directory* which are available at most public libraries. News-America asks for three weeks worth of material, be it columns or cartoons. The firm reports back in 10 to 12 weeks as to whether the material has been accepted. Syndication fees depend on how often the material is to appear and how many outlets have purchased it.

Once syndicated, it is incumbent upon you as writer or cartoonist to maintain the high level of work that got your efforts noticed in the first place.

80 Tall Ship Crew Member

The sea . . . the sea . . . Since man first floated a log down a stream, the oceans of the world have beckoned him. For centuries the seas were traversed by square-rigged sailing ships with canvases billowing under a full wind. Some of the world's greatest novels were written during the age of sail, and it is small wonder, since few other experiences test man and his spirit more than 30-foot waves and gale force winds.

The age of sail still exists and it still calls men and women with its siren song. On the East Coast alone there are over 20 sailing vessels that either carry passengers on nautical vacations (the *Mystic Clipper*), serve as ambassadors for a region (the *Spirit of Massachusetts*), or serve as alternative treatment programs for delinquent youths (the *Western Union*). A complete listing of tall ships, their home ports and captains can be obtained by writing to the:

American Sail Training Association
Newport Harbor Center
365 Thames Street
Newport, RI 02840

Being a deckhand on a schooner or other tall-masted sailing ship involves a lot of desire, some small boat experience, and the ability to meet the discerning standards of the ship's master. "I'll take someone off the dock if he looks good instead of worrying about some six-page resume," said Quentin Snediker, captain of the *Mystic Clipper.*

Crew members usually work 10 to 12 hours a day depending on the watch system, and cruise durations can last up to an entire year depending on the purpose of the vessel. On-board experience takes care of learning the various lines and sails needed to maneuver a large vessel. Salaries average about $100 per week plus room and board on the ship.

Snediker said the romance of crewing on a schooner soon disappears after you have to unplug a stopped toilet or perform some other dirty, exhausting task. Drowning is a distinct possibility. In 1986, the *Pride of Baltimore* sank (it is now being rebuilt) during a freak storm and several crew members lost their lives. Still, the job is much in demand.

If you love ships and want to work closely with nature, there may be an available berth. Being at the right place at the right time has a lot to do with it; so does volunteering time to assist the various groups that sponsor tall ships. Robin Carrig spent seven years behind a desk at a public relations firm before she started to frequent the yard where the *Spirit of Massachusetts* was being built. Finally, somebody stuck a broom in her hand and said, "Get to work." She has been sailing the Atlantic Coast for over a year, now.

As Snediker said, "This job lets you live more at the extremes of life. Your job, hobby, and life are all wrapped together as one."

81 Tattoo Artist

Contrary to popular belief, the art of tattooing did not begin with the founding of the Marine Corps. Many cultures throughout history have used tattoos as a way of proclaiming prowess in battle, lineage of chieftains, and eternal love for mother.

Modern tattooists have been able to refine this venerable tradition by incorporating into their designs a wider array of coloring agents. A tattoo no longer needs to be a dull green blur. When sketched over a large area of the body it can in fact be stunning.

A tattoo is applied by first swabbing the chosen part of the body with alcohol and then using a stencil to mark out the pattern. A tattooing "pen" with a high speed vibrating needle is used next to etch out the pattern and to inject the pigments below the skin. Different sized needles are used for different purposes–narrow ones for drawing lines, and broader ones for shading and working colors into the skin. A properly drawn tattoo usually lasts 10 years before it needs retouching.

Although the process is rather straightforward, tattooist Louie Lombi said there is "more to it than meets the eye." In addition to skill as an artist, Lombi said, a tattooist must know about anatomy, muscle tension, skin texture, pigmentation, and chemistry. For instance, he explained that mixing blue and red pigments normally produce purple. But when applied to certain types of skin the pigments turn brown.

To learn these subtleties, a tattooist undergoes an apprenticeship for several years. A novice should find somebody whose work commands respect and who is also willing to teach. High-calibre tatooists can be located through the:

Professional Tattoo Artists Guild
198 West First Street
Mt. Vernon, NY 10550

During the apprenticeship, Lombi said, you will rarely if ever administer a tattoo. Instead, time is spent cleaning up the shop, assembling needles, and performing sterilization tasks. All the while, however, you should be watching, learning, and asking questions. "You learn from the ground up. The method is designed to allow you to see how committed you are to becoming a tattooist," Lombi said.

Once you have the basic knowledge of tattooing, the next step is to overcome the nervousness of applying a tattoo. "You learn right away how to fix mistakes," Lombi noted. A top-notch tattooist can develop a nationwide clientele, especially if the artist is skilled at freehand drawing. Individual prices vary, but a stencil tattoo usually averages between $50 and $100. People from all walks of life, women included, are attracted to tattoos. For them, beauty is just slightly more than skin deep.

82 Texas Ranger

Most folks outside of Texas have the Texas Rangers freeze-framed in the era of gunslingers and stagecoach bandits. But these cops have kept pace with the times and there are still Texas Rangers. The modern Ranger organization is a 94-member force with statewide jurisdiction.

To become a Texas Ranger, you need not be a native of Texas but you do need to have at least eight years of law enforcement experience, with the last two as an officer for the Texas Department of Public Safety. Once you have the necessary experience, you can apply to take the Ranger's annual test by writing to the:

Texas Department of Public Safety
Austin, TX 78773

The top 30 scorers on the written test must then undergo a difficult oral interview with two Ranger captains and other Department of Public Safety officials. The candidates are grilled for their knowledge of Texas law and police investigative techniques. The five leading candidates who pass the interview board are then placed on a one-year eligibility list. If openings occur due to resignations or retirements, they will be filled from this list. If there are no openings, you must re-apply the following year.

Once you have been admitted to the force, you will be assigned to one of the five Ranger companies located around the state. Since Rangers are not bound by local jurisdiction, you will be free to "range" over several county-wide areas to assist local police with the investigation of major crimes, the apprehension of fugitives, the suppression of riots, and the protection of life and property. You may also continue an investigation in any part of the United States with the approval of the Public Safety Director.

Rangers must be a versatile lot. The resources of the state crime laboratories are at their disposal, so they must have full knowledge of modern investigative techniques. Since Texas still has large amounts of ranchland, they must also be skilled at horsemanship to track down cattle rustlers. Saddles and spurs are as much a part of Ranger equipment as are high-intensity spotlights.

Each Ranger is required to submit to headquarters a weekly written report indicating total hours worked and comments about ongoing investigations. For his efforts, a Ranger receives $27,700 a year plus a per diem and clothing allowance.

The Texas Rangers are extremely proud of their traditions, and their exploits have been recounted in many an adventure book. They still wear Stetsons and, when the occasion warrants it, strap on two-holster gun belts holding Colt Frontier .45s. Given the size of Texas and its burgeoning population, there really aren't that many Texas Rangers to go around. But from the Ranger viewpoint, the quality of the force far exceeds its quantity.

83 Toll Collector

You do it for money and job security.

This, in a nutshell, is what draws people to the task of collecting fees at turnpikes and toll plazas across the country. As a civil service position, toll collectors have their jobs and salaries protected by law. With overtime, some earn in the area of $30,000 per year, although the average range is in the teens to mid-twenties.

A high school diploma is usually required, and those who pass the civil service test can start working after a short training period that familiarizes the collector with the different fee structures for cars and trucks.

A person's attitude affects how quickly time passes in the booth. One collector said cheerfulness makes the time fly. "A driver likes to see a smile and it makes me feel good too," she said. Some jurisdictions also invest their collectors with peace officer status, so collectors are on the lookout for drunk drivers and stolen vehicles. Exhaust fumes are a distinct drawback of this profession. The Triborough Authority in New York, for instance, gives its collectors "air release breaks" to mitigate the effects of bad air.

There are over 5,000 miles of toll roads, bridges, and tunnels in the United States, covering over 200 jurisdictions, so there are plenty of positions to be filled. Those interested in applying for a job as toll collector should contact their city and state personnel offices to see when the next series of exams is being given.

84 Translator

An adept translator can say "no problem" in English as well as in a foreign language. The translator is the human element in the worldwide communications network. It is their job to insure that the accuracy of a message equals the speed of its delivery.

The profession of dealing with foreign languages can be broken into two fields–interpretation and translation. For the most part, interpretation means dealing with oral communications such as the simultaneous rendering of diplomatic speeches that is done at the United Nations. Translation means dealing with printed matter such as technical manuals.

For interpreters, a great deal of training is needed to facilitate listening to a foreign language and turning it into English. "A person just has to fly with it," said Mrs. Sue Ellen Wright, a member of the American Translators Association (ATA). The results can be challenging and exciting since an interpreter can be at the center of history-making events between heads of state.

The three leading schools that provide interpreter training are:

State University of New York at Binghamton
Binghamton, NY 13902

Monterey Institute of International Studies
Department of Translation and Interpretation
P.O. Box 1978
Monterey, CA 93940

School of Languages and Linguistics
Division of Interpretation and Translation
Georgetown University
Washington, DC 20007

One of the major employers of interpreters is the United Nations, and the department that oversees their placement is the:

Recruitment Programmes Section
Office of Personnel Services
United Nations
New York, NY 10017

As for translators, there are several approaches to the profession. The first is through the military language training programs. A second is through mastering a technical field such as computer science and then studying a foreign language to complement it.

Mrs. Wright said the major demand for translation work is connected with technical manuals and scientific papers. "A translator must first have a keen sense of technical writing in his or her native language and then apply it to the foreign one," she noted. The major fields that will require translation work in the future are engineering, medicine, law, computer science, and the "hard" sciences such as physics and biology, especially where it concerns genetic research. The languages that will be most in demand are Japanese, Chinese, and Arabic.

Once a translator receives his or her training, the next step is to become accredited with the ATA. The address is:

American Translators Association
109 Croton Avenue
Ossining, NY 10562

The association administers competency tests in a variety of foreign languages and also maintains a registry of translators along with their respective skills. Mrs. Wright said both government and industry make use of in-house and freelance translators. Companies that maintain in-house staffs include IBM, Bell Laboratories, Sperry Corporation, and the Siemens Corporation. Freelancers act as independent business consultants and garner assignments by advertising in the ATA journal and through personal contacts.

People who do well at translation work love languages and are attentive to detail. Being a member of an ethnic group or having a bilingual background also helps. Translators earn between $20,000 and $50,000 per year depending on the difficulty of their assignments.

85 Windsmith

On a California wind farm, you'll find nary a tumbleweed. Instead, rising above the brown earth are rows of spidery steel towers supporting the powerful wind generators that account for 1 percent of California's supply of electricity. Servicing the nearly 15,000 generators in the state are crews of windsmiths, a novel name for a unique profession that will grow in demand as the world turns its attention to nonpolluting sources of energy.

Windsmiths are individuals who have a background in mechanics or construction. They enjoy working out of doors and do not mind heights or dangerous conditions–i.e., servicing a seven-ton generator mounted up 60 to 140 feet high. Servicing a wind generator is similar to maintaining a diesel tractor. Brake pads must be replaced, transmission fluid changed, and a general "nuts and bolts" inspection undertaken on a quarterly basis.

For their efforts, windsmiths average about $10 per hour, and are likely to work for one of the following firms–U.S. Windpower, Fayette Manufacturing, Zond Systems, Flo-Wind, Inc., or Seawest. These firms are centered in the three major sites of California wind production, Altamont Pass, Tehachapi, and San Gorgonio. Nearly 85 percent of the world's wind energy is generated at these locations with another 10 percent produced in Denmark, according to Paul Gibe of the American Wind Energy Institute.

Effective wind energy depends on an average wind speed of 11 miles per hour. There are several states in the Midwest that also fit this requirement. It is one of the reasons the Red Wing Technical Institute in Red Wing, Minnesota has instituted a wind energy education center.

Gibe said the Red Wing school is one of the foremost in the country for training managerial staff at wind farms. For more information, write to the:

Red Wing Energy Education Center
c/o Red Wing Technical Institute
Highways 61 and 19 West
Red Wing, MN 55066

During their first year at school, students undergo a general education curriculum which stresses physics and electronics. During their second year they have the option of concentrating on wind energy applications.

Gibe said that although the work is risky, being a windsmith gives you a sense of accomplishment and pride that comes from doing more about creating a benign source of energy than simply shooting the breeze.

86 Wine Steward

Whoever coined the phrase, "Let there be wine, women, and song," truly had the priorities of a wine steward. For, although women may prove fickle, and songs can be played off-key, the pleasure associated with a good bottle of wine can always be counted upon.

Wine stewards, or sommeliers, are grand masters of the grape, and their knowledge of the vast world of wines is sought after by quality hotels and restaurants.

A wine steward does not need an innate sixth sense to assist in rating the quality of wines. This attunement of the taste buds comes through education and experience. Indeed, the first step in becoming a wine steward is to familiarize yourself with the restaurant industry, according to sommelier Paul Margulies of New York City. "You have to know everything that everyone knows, plus wines," he observed.

As for learning about wines, this can be accomplished through reading on the subject, attending wine tastings, and taking formal classes. A formal course is offered by the:

Sommelier Society of America
435 Fifth Avenue
New York, NY 10016

The Society's 25-session course features such topics as aperitifs, lesser known wines of the world, German wines, and California wines. You can find out about classes in other parts of the country by perusing the magazine *Wine Spectator.*

Through the comparison of traits, the erudite phrases associated with wine tasting assume a practical meaning. Beginning sommeliers should also learn the refinements of serving wine, such as how to take an order and how to open and serve a bottle for a dinner guest. With solid training, a sommelier in a major urban area can earn up to $50,000 per year through tips and salary. In addition to being directly involved with a restaurant's clientele, wine stewards may manage the wine cellar for a hotel or restaurant. Further opportunities avail themselves in the fields of teaching wine classes or acting as vineyard sales representatives.

Before you order a matching set of corkscrews, remember that each harvest season brings a whole new set of vintages with which a sommelier must become familiar. A wine steward is not really experienced until several hundred wines are committed to memory. A sense of showmanship also helps. "Forget the snobby stuff," Margulies said. "A wine steward should be part entertainer and have common sense and a good sense of humor."

87 Wing Walker

During the heyday of aerial barnstorming, during the late 1920s and 1930s, wing walkers drew gasps of awe and delight from county fair crowds by playing banjos, holding pie fights, and making human pyramids while perched on the top wing of a Curtiss Jenny biplane.

It may come as a surprise that, in this age of supersonic jet travel, wing walkers are still walking at an airport in rural Virginia.

"They don't do it for the money, that's for sure," said Charley Kulp, one of the founders of the Flying Circus. "Wing walking triggers something inside a person. It gets the adrenaline flowing. We only take on people who have already had rappeling, parachuting, or mountain climbing experience. We don't want folks who are just doing it on a whim. We want someone who will be with us for a while."

If you meet this character assessment, you can work with a veteran wing walker to learn how to climb out of the cockpit and onto the wing. When this ground training is completed, you take off and, as Kulp said, "They either do it or they don't"

Wing walkers earn $50 plying their trade every Sunday, from May to October, during an afternoon air show. The show is held at

The Flying Circus
Bealeton, VA

Kulp said that anyone who desires to wing walk

should visit the airfield and talk to some of the wing walkers before coming to a decision. "Everyone always asks 'What happens if you fall?' Well, one of our fellows simply says, 'You die.'"

88 Yacht Crew Member

Bora Bora . . . Tonga . . . Samoa . . . There is a society of men and women who call these ports of call home. No jet-setters these folks–they are instead sail-setters. At any given time, there are thousands of people following the winds in 38- to 45-foot long sailing yachts to the far reaches of the globe. There is an excellent chance that they need crew members to assist them in their travels.

If you are seeking adventure on the high seas, or long to spend time in some of the world's more romantic settings, then here is the way to circumnavigate the world and satisfy your desires at a reasonable cost. Often, during a planned sailing voyage, one of the original crew may need to return home. This leaves a boat short-handed, and the skipper has to fill the empty slot. The fastest solution is to see who is available in port for the next leg of the journey.

As a prospective crew member, then, you need to be at the right place at the right time. It helps to discover this juncture by talking to everyone around the marina. Dockmasters, yard workers, and yacht club members are helpful. A few evenings spent at the local watering hole may also prove illuminating.

It pays to have at least taken the free U.S. Coast Guard Sailing and Seamanship courses. These courses are offered around the country, and the nearest one can be located by calling 800-336-2628. The more sailing skills you have, the better. Other valuable assets are the ability to cook, fix engines, and navigate. Yacht crew members do not simply go along for the ride.

While you're in port, you should be sizing up the boat, crew, and skipper. Do the other crew members smoke? Are they teetotalers? Are there adequate safety rafts and foul-weather harnesses? Women should also discreetly determine if a male skipper wants more than just a crew member. In other words a boat is small, the journey is long, and if people aren't compatible, a sailboat can become a floating pressure cooker.

Ports that have a good share of long distance sailing vessels include Camden, Maine; Marblehead, Nantucket, Edgartown, and Woods Hole, Massachusetts; Newport, Rhode Island; Annapolis, Maryland; Clearwater, Key West, and Ft. Lauderdale, Florida; and San Francisco, Los Angeles, San Diego, and Marina del Rey, California. An alternative to visiting a port is to peruse magazines such as *Cruising World* and *Yachting*. Use their classified ad sections to locate skippers or to advertise your services. There are also listings for agencies that match skippers and crews.

Once aboard, be prepared to travel light. A small duffel containing foul-weather gear, swimsuits, and a few changes of clothes should suffice. You will probably not be paid as a crew member, but then again, there is no way to spend money when you're out at sea 200 miles west of Guam.

As for finances, a year of cruising expenses should be in the neighborhood of $2,000. Be prepared to come ashore with enough money to fly home or plan on seeking work to replenish the bankroll. In American ports such as Samoa, you can work legally, but in foreign ports, it has to be under the table. Mechanics and cooks are always needed, as are entertainers. Before sailing, learn enough magic tricks to perform a show and use the world as a stage.

More great career books from Ten Speed Press

WHAT COLOR IS YOUR PARACHUTE? by Richard N. Bolles

This classic in the career field is substantially revised and updated every year. Practical advice, step-by-step exercises, and a warm, human tone make it *the* guide for job-hunters and career changers. "The giant title in the field"—*The New York Times* $12.95 paper, 448 pages

WHO'S HIRING WHO by Richard Lathrop

Fully revised and updated version of a career book highly recommended by Richard Bolles. Practical, hands-on methods for scouting the job market, presenting any and all experience in the best light, and landing the right job at the right salary. $9.95 paper, 268 pages

THE DAMN GOOD RESUME GUIDE by Yana Parker

Our bestselling resume book, updated with 22 all-new functional-style resumes (perfect for those with offbeat job histories). Shows how to turn your resume into a vital self-marketing tool, not just a boring list of jobs. Sections on informational interviewing, targeting your resume to your job objective, and integrating work and nonwork experience. $6.95 paper, 80 pages

THE OVERNIGHT RÉSUMÉ by Donald Asher

Tricks of the trade from the president of Résumé Righters (the largest resume-writing office in the world) enable anyone to write a hard-hitting, fast-track resume overnight. Special sections on common resume problems and how to avoid them, job search protocol, and unique resume styles—medical, law, finance, and academic. $7.95 paper, 136 pages

DYNAMIC COVER LETTERS by Katherine Hansen

Too often, people put all of their creative energy into writing a great resume and then send it off with a lackluster cover letter. The savvy marketing tips, simple charts and exercises, and over fifty examples of real letters in this book allow anyone to create a dynamic, effective cover letter. $7.95 paper, 96 pages

Available from your local bookstore, or order direct from the publisher.
Please include $1.25 shipping & handling for the first book,
and 50 cents for each additional book. California residents include local sales tax.
Write for our free complete catalog of over 400 books and tapes.

TEN SPEED PRESS

Box 7123   Berkeley, California 94707